GUIDANCE
from God's Word

GUIDANCE
from God's Word

A 40-Day Devotional Journey

Peter Horrobin

Sovereign World

Published by
Sovereign World Ltd
Ellel Grange
Bay Horse
Lancaster
LA2 0HN
United Kingdom

www.sovereignworld.com

Twitter: @sovereignworld
Facebook: www.facebook.com/sovereignworld

Published October 2019

ISBN
978-1-85240-846-6 (print)
978-1-85240-851-0 (epub)
978-1 85240-856 5-(kindle)

British Library Cataloguing-in-Publication Data
A catalogue record for this book is available from the British Library.

Typeset by Avocet Typeset, Bideford, Devon, EX39 2BP
Printed in Great Britain by Bell & Bain Ltd, Glasgow

Contents

Contents

Introduction

Guidance

We all need the guidance of God in our lives. Guidance is a topic of great importance for the Christian who wants to do the will of God and fulfil their destiny as a follower of Jesus. Thankfully, it's also a topic of huge importance to God. Otherwise, there wouldn't be so many relevant scriptures in the Bible which the Holy Spirit can use to help us live the Christian life.

God has given us free-will, and He rejoices to see us enjoying the freedom that is ours, because that is how He made us to be. I passionately believe that God has also given each one of us a purpose and a destiny. When we use our free-will to choose to walk in the way He has prepared for us, then we will know the greatest joy, fulfilment and contentment that it is possible to experience.

In the Scriptures, God tells us many times that He will guide His people. Jesus told us that when 'the Spirit of truth, comes, he will guide you into all truth' (John 16:13).

In Exodus 15:13 we read, 'In your unfailing love you will lead the people you have redeemed. In your strength you will guide them.' Then Nehemiah expresses this great truth by describing how God led His people from Egypt to the promised land:

'Because of your great compassion you did not abandon them in the wilderness. By day the pillar of cloud did not fail to **guide** them on their path, nor the pillar of fire by night to **shine on the way** they were to take' (Nehemiah 9:19) (my emphasis).

While we may not be privileged to have the pillar of cloud and the pillar of fire which were essential to guide millions of Jews along a path they hadn't trodden before, God has, since then, given us His written Word to guide and direct our steps. He is full of compassion towards all those who love Him and choose to follow Him. In Psalm 119:14-16 we read:

'I rejoice in following your statutes as one rejoices in great riches. I meditate upon your precepts and consider your ways. I delight in your decrees; I will not neglect your word.'

Here the law of God is described as great riches. It is a fact that, when people choose to follow God's ways and honour His covenant, then He promises them His blessing: 'The LORD will send a blessing on your barns and on everything you put your hand to' (Deuteronomy 28:8).

In Psalm 119:105, the Psalmist describes the law of God,

which is contained in the first five books of our Bible, as a 'lamp to my feet and a light to my path.' This is a really important scripture, for it underlines a foundational principle of Christian living – guidance is simply knowing where to place my feet next on the path of life – one step at a time! Whilst we may like to have neon lights in the sky or massive signposts pointing us to our eventual destination, this is not how God usually operates.

He may give us a vision to fulfil, but we don't suddenly jump from here to there – for there are steps to be taken along the way towards our destination, as we learn to discern His voice and trust that He knows best. The biggest mistake I ever made in my business career was when I knew what God was saying, but I chose to do the opposite. It was a very costly mistake. Conversely, when I have chosen to do what I was sensing God was saying, it has always proved to be the very best decision I could have ever made.

Those who have achieved great things for God have only ever been able to take one step at a time as, hand in hand with the Lord, they have been building the Kingdom of God in the particular area of God's vineyard in which He has planted them. At the time they didn't usually know how important the next step they took would be, but when they looked back they could see how obedience in the seemingly little things had opened the door to so much more. Huge doors swing open on small hinges.

So, in tackling this vital topic of guidance in this devotional volume, you won't find massive signposts telling you which way to go. But you will discover the basic principles through which we are enabled to put our feet down each day in the right place – and learn how to avoid putting our feet down on the enemy's minefield, which he carefully constructs to try and blow us off course!

I pray that as you work through the pages of this book over the next forty days that you will sense the hand of God guiding and directing your life and preparing you for the destiny that He has stored up for you.

How to use this book

This book has been laid out as a 40-step journey of faith. It was designed to be read little by little, one day at a time. Before you begin to read each day's scripture and the devotional reading, I would encourage you to spend a few moments in prayer – lay aside all the concerns of the moment and ask the Holy Spirit to open up God's Word to you and to minister His truth into your inner being.

Then read the Bible text for the day – not once, but two or three times, allowing God to speak to you personally through the words from Scripture. Next, read the devotional with an open heart, asking God to show you how what is said can relate to events and circumstances in your own life. You may find it helpful to read the devotional through again.

At the end of each devotional is a suggested prayer which will help you anchor the daily truths into the reality of your own life. But I would encourage you to pray more personally as well, applying to your own situation whatever God has said to you through the devotional.

Finally, there is a space for you to make your own personal comments about the scripture and the devotional and to keep a record of what God says to you. It has always been a huge encouragement to me to look back at the things God has said or done in the past to trace the record of God's hand on my life.

I pray that this little book will be a rich blessing to you and that as you move on with God you will know His presence and empowering day by day as He directs your steps.

Peter Horrobin
September 2019

Day 1

The Plans of God

'"For I know the plans I have for you," declares the LORD, "plans to prosper you and not to harm you, plans to give you a hope and a future. Then you will call upon me and come and pray to me, and I will listen to you. You will seek me and find me when you seek me with all your heart."' Jeremiah 29:11

It's hugely encouraging to begin our 40-day devotional journey with a scripture which powerfully affirms that God has plans for His people – plans to give them a hope and a future. And, that He wants to hear and answer our prayers. He wants to show us where to put our feet down and guide us on our journey through life.

The words of our scripture were originally spoken to God's people when they were in exile in Babylon. They had been in rebellion against God, lost their protection and had been taken prisoner. They had ceased to listen to God's voice, had gone their own way and were now suffering the consequences of their mistakes. They were a long way off track. We can sometimes find ourselves in a similar situation.

It was into this situation that God sent His prophet Jeremiah to speak encouragement and to tell them that, despite the mess they were now in, God still had plans for them. He still loved them, His eye was still on them and He wanted to lead them back home and into their eventual destiny as God's chosen people.

But how could He do that? How could God guide and direct His people when they were in such a devastating situation? The key lies in the last sentence of our scripture, where God says, '"You will seek me and find me when you seek me with all your heart."'

All journeys have a beginning. The beginning of our own journey of discovery, as we look to Him for guidance and direction in our lives, has to be with exactly the same intent – a determination to seek the Lord with *all our heart*. When we do that, God promises to listen to our prayers and to start showing us His plans – plans that will give us hope and lead us into the future that He has prepared for us.

If that is something that God could do for His people when they were still prisoners in physical captivity, no-one can ever say that their own situation is too difficult for Him, or beyond His capacity to help them. We are all included in the plans and purposes of God if we want to be.

Many people don't feel free to follow God's guidance and direction because they are still prisoners to their past. Some have been so hurt by things that have happened that they feel God has overlooked them, and they are unworthy of His love. Others are not able to seek God with all their heart because they are guarding ungodly things in their heart that they want to hang on to or holding secrets they are ashamed of.

From God's point of view, none of these things, or the many other possible obstacles, can ever turn His heart away from the people He created and loved. As we journey together through these devotionals, we will see how every single one of us can come to God without fear and with an open heart to receive His direction. His plans are to prosper our lives and not to harm us, to give us a hope and a future!

Prayer: *Thank You, Lord, that Your love for me is unconditional. I want to seek You with all my heart. Help me to face the reality of anything hidden that needs to come into the light and to forgive those who have hurt me so that I can start to trust again. Lord, I come to You with everything I am and pray that You will show me your plans for my life. In Jesus' name, Amen.*

Personal Notes

Day 2

Show Me Your Ways, O Lord

'Show me your ways, O LORD, teach me your paths; guide me in your truth and teach me, for you are GOD my Saviour, and my hope is in you all day long.' Psalm 25:4-5

This prayer of David contains three foundational requests. In it he is looking to God and saying: **Show me – Teach me – Guide me.**

We learn by seeing, we learn by hearing and we then follow our Guide, the one who is showing us the way to go. Before we are in a place where we can hear the directions the Lord would have us take, however, we first need to learn about the ways of the Lord and be taught how to follow in His footsteps.

Ultimately, the simplest key to guidance is learning how

to put your feet down in the place where God has already planted His – so that you are walking in His footprints. This is how Moses led the Children of Israel through the wilderness to the promised land. He watched what God was doing by following the pillars of cloud and fire. Then, in Exodus 33:15, Moses said, "'If your Presence does not go with us, do not send us up from here.'" Moses had learnt the vital lesson that to be anywhere else but in the presence of God would mean they were going off course!

I recently visited the bridge of a ship and listened to the captain explaining the intricacies of navigation. He explained how the safe passage of the ship through the oceans did not only depend on the navigators who plotted the course of the ship, but also on the crew who were responsible for acting on the information supplied by the navigators. Obedience to the instructions then became the absolute key to the safety of the vessel and to reaching the ship's expected destination.

In today's scripture we are encouraged to come to the Lord for His navigational instructions – we want to know what path He has prepared for us in the next season of our lives. Without His guidance we will always finish up a long way away from His best plan for the way ahead.

But, and this is a big BUT, although we may know exactly what the Lord would have us do, if we choose not to follow His navigational instructions and do our own thing, then we will soon be in trouble and make a shipwreck of our lives. After making an amazing cross-Atlantic voyage in his ship *Santa Maria*, Christopher Columbus and his key crew members were exhausted and in need of sleep. They left the ship in the charge of a young boy, but unfortunately this lad did not follow his instructions and, as a result, the ship foundered on a sandbank and was lost!

We cannot afford to allow anyone other than the Lord to be the Navigator who shows us the direction we need to go. And we cannot allow anyone else to take control of our lives and take us to places God never intended for us. Learning to always trust Him and be obedient to His directions is the primary key to having the blessing of God on each and every area of our lives and on each stage of the journey that lies ahead.

Prayer: *Thank You, Lord, that You rejoice to be the navigator of our lives. Help me, Lord, not only to listen to Your voice but to obey Your instructions. I do not want to find myself away from Your presence, so please show me where You are planting Your feet so that I can walk in Your footprints. In Jesus' name, Amen.*

Personal Notes

Day 3

Hearing the Voice of the Lord

'The LORD confides in those who fear him; he makes his covenant known to them. My eyes are ever on the LORD, for only he will release my feet from the snare.' Psalm 25:14

When you confide in someone, you are doing two things. Firstly, you are trusting them and secondly, you are sharing with them things that are private to you. This remarkable verse expresses an incredible and amazing truth – that the living God, the Creator of the Universe, wants to trust us and share with each one of us personally in just this way!

He wants to share with us things that are precious, things that are important to us, that are not for anyone else to hear, and which will show us the way He wants us to go. This is the heart of guidance – God's way! But, if we want to be one of those who are able to hear the Lord guiding us like this, then there is a condition that we need to fulfil.

The key lies in having a holy fear of the Lord – not the sort of fear that makes us shake with fright, but the sort of fear which comes from respect, reverence and awe and which, ultimately, directs our choices through love, so that our desire is always to please Him. This does not mean that we stop being our own person, but that God rejoices when we are free to be the person He made us to be – able to be blessed by Him and be a blessing to others.

Hebrews 11:7 tells us that it was in holy fear that Noah built the ark – it was vital for Noah to be constantly hearing the Lord's voice, guiding and directing him in the building of the most important ship that humanity has ever known. It saved the human race! To fear Him means that you will always want to follow and obey Him because you love Him! Those who truly love Him show their love by wanting to walk in His ways. Their first choice will always be to do those things that please Him. Jesus said, "'If you love me, keep my commands'" (John 14:15).

Someone who walks in the fear of the Lord will not need to be concerned lest they accidentally transgress the commandments of God, for the Lord's gentle confiding voice will show them what is right and what is wrong. It is through this profound principle of what it means to be in a covenant relationship with God, that we can enjoy the guidance of the Lord in all of life's many different circumstances.

Then the promise of the second part of the verse can be fulfilled. When our eyes are on Him, He is able to warn us of snares laid on our pathway by the enemy of souls. No wonder Isaiah said that the Sovereign Lord would come to 'proclaim freedom for the captives' (Isaiah 61:1). Many is the person I have prayed with who has taken the bait of the enemy and finished up ensnared, hobbling through life, injured by being in the enemy's spiritual trap.

If, however, we do get caught in the enemy's snare, the psalmist tells us how we can hear God's voice, showing us how to escape. We can't change the fact that we have been in a snare, but God delights to set us free and heal us, so that once again we can step forward on the journey of life going in the right direction.

If there has been sin, then we need to confess it. If there is hurt caused by others we need to forgive them and receive the Lord's healing. If we have walked away from God's plans for our life, we need to tell the Lord we love Him and ask Him to help us get back on track. As we keep our eyes fixed firmly on Him, He will lead and direct our steps. For, as the psalmist says in Psalm 119:44-45, 'I will walk about in freedom for I have sought out your precepts.'

Prayer: *Lord, I would love to hear Your confiding voice sharing with me Your truths and leading me along the path of righteousness. Help me, Lord, to listen carefully to what You share with me, to seek out Your precepts and walk in them. Help me to desire above all else to walk day by day within the* *provisions of Your covenant blessings. Please show me how to escape the snares of the enemy, follow and obey You all my days. I love You, Lord. In Jesus' name, Amen.*

Personal Notes

Day 4

Light in the Darkness

'Through him all things were made; without him nothing was made that has been made. In him was life and that life was the light of mankind. The light shines in the darkness, but the darkness has not understood it.' John 1:3-5

Isaiah prophesied that the people who are walking in darkness would see a great light and that this light would dawn on those living in the land of the shadow of death (Isaiah 9:2). John, knowing that Jesus described himself as the Light of the World (John 8:12), began his gospel by picking up on Isaiah's prophecy and declaring the amazing truth that we read about in today's scripture – THE light has come!

Isaiah saw the light coming, like the headlamp of a distant train speeding down the centuries on the track of time. John saw the light arrive and then watched it speeding further down the track of time into the future. For all generations since, Jesus has not only been the Light of the World but also, as John expressed it, the light of mankind. Jesus is the light for all generations of people who choose to believe in Him. His light shines into the darkness of our sinful lives and transforms us from the inside out.

Later in the chapter, John expresses the amazing truth that all who receive Him and believe in His name have the right to become children of God – born afresh into His wonderful Kingdom. Tragically, not everyone wants His light. John spoke so accurately when he said that the darkness would not understand the light. The simple fact is, we live in an increasingly dark world – a world which is becoming less and less interested in the truths of scripture and more and more tolerant of spiritual darkness.

The way of life of those who choose to live in spiritual darkness is challenged by the life and the teaching of the Son of God. What Jesus says, on so many different issues, stands in sharp contrast to what people want to hear. The god of this world has blinded their eyes and dulled their understanding. They don't want to receive either correction or direction, for pride says "I'm OK, thank you very much! I know where I'm going!" They don't want to know about sin and the reality of eternal judgment and death.

If you don't understand what's happening when darkness becomes your normal way of life, then you won't be looking for the light which can lead you away from death and into the new life which God offers to all who will believe in His Son. A devotional series on guidance is a wonderful opportunity to remind yourself of who Jesus really is, to choose life instead of death and to welcome Him, the Light of the World, into your life.

Without a guide we will soon get lost. Without a light we will never be able to see the way. The ultimate key to guidance in the Christian life is never to lose sight of the Guide and to always be aware that He is the living Word, the One who will be 'a lamp to my feet and a light to my path' (Psalm 119:105).

Prayer: *Thank You, Jesus, for being the Light of the World and for being the light of all those who receive You as Saviour and Lord. Today, Lord Jesus, I welcome You into my life and invite you to shine Your light into every corner of my being, so that I may see myself as You see me, receive forgiveness and healing, and step forward in faith and trust to live all my days in Your service. In Your name I pray, Amen.*

Personal Notes

Day 5

The Purposes of God for YOU!

'For we are God's workmanship, created in Christ Jesus to do good works, which God prepared in advance for us to do.'
Ephesians 2:10

I love making things and have made many different things in my life – ranging from bookshelves to toys. I learnt the art of making things from my Dad, who clearly enjoyed making things for different members of the family. Every Christmas he would present Mum with a new piece of furniture which he had lovingly made. The joy of creating things for a purpose – things which we have thought about, designed and then completed – is very deep-seated in the heart of man.

The reason why we get such joy out of making things like this is because, as God's children, we are a direct reflection of our Heavenly Father – the ultimate Creator. God is good and, therefore, as God's workmanship, we are also designed to do good works. Our salvation comes through faith – but as redeemed sinners we now have a new nature, and from this comes the desire to do good works.

Just as when we make things, we create them to fulfil a purpose, God has created each one of us with a purpose to live for. It is as we follow Him, day by day, that we gradually discover the good works that He has created us to do – the things that He prepared for us in advance. This advance preparation is an expression of God's wonderful providence. He has gifted each of us with different desires, gifts and abilities so that we can uniquely fulfil the purposes that He has laid before us and know the joy of walking in our destiny.

There are no exceptions – God has created each and every one of us for a purpose and today we can each rejoice in the amazing blessing of knowing that the deepest joy of our lives will be experienced as we discover and do those good things God has prepared for us.

The essence of guidance in the Christian life, therefore, is to discover the things that we are best equipped to do and the direction that our heavenly Father wishes us to take through our lives. As a Father He doesn't want us to be pressed into someone else's mould, but to become the special individual that He planned in the first place.

I will never forget the doctor who had to retire on health grounds at a very young age. Throughout his career he had been hounded by depression caused by a deep-seated hatred of his job. His father had always wanted to be a doctor but, because of the war, had never had the opportunity. He had therefore made a vow that, if he ever had a son, the boy would grow up to be the doctor he could never be. But this wasn't what his son wanted. Healing came only when the young doctor left his medical career, forgave his father and began to seek afresh God's new destiny for him. God is a healer and a restorer and He can make all things new.

Prayer: *Thank You, Lord, for Your amazing love and for preparing good things for me to enjoy doing. Help me to discover the gifts You have given me so that I can use them to Your glory. In the name of Jesus, Amen.*

Personal Notes

Day 6

The Beginning of Wisdom

'The fear of the LORD is the beginning of wisdom, and knowledge of the Holy One is understanding. For through me your days will be many, and years will be added to your life.' Proverbs 9:10-11

Everyone would like to live longer! Here, in this scripture is one of the primary keys for extending the days of our life. But it is not a key that too many people want to use, for using it requires a determination to make sure that God has priority in all of life's choices. The carnal nature and the ways of the world are always opposed to the ways of God and obedience to the Word of God is always at odds with the desires of the flesh.

I frequently hear or read of people whose lives were tragically terminated in needless accidents from driving when under the influence of alcohol, or through drugs or a disease that was contracted as a result of their ungodly lifestyle. It is easy to see how such people would have lived a lot longer if a holy fear of grieving the God who loves them had been the motivation of their life choices and God had become their Guide for life.

On occasions I have been asked, "If you only had one sermon left to preach, what would you speak on?" My answer has always been Exodus 20:20. A person with 20-20 vision is said to have perfect eyesight, and in Exodus 20:20 we have the key to perfect spiritual sight. For it is here that we read, 'the fear of God will be with you to keep you from sinning.'

In the immediate presence of the living God no-one would think of sinning. And most people would be mounting a rear-guard action to try and cover up any evidence of past misdemeanours! The holiness of God exposes darkness and repels the enemy. One of the best definitions I know of holy fear is living as if God Himself is sitting with you in the room and being conscious of His presence wherever you go.

But God really is with us wherever we are and wherever we go. And when people know and love the Lord and have a knowledge of Him and His ways, then holy fear will make them want to carefully plan their lives according to the His will, for this will be their desire and their joy. As Nehemiah said, 'the joy of the LORD shall be your strength' (Nehemiah 8:10).

When we truly walk in the ways of God, then the days of our life are surely in the hands of the Lord. But if we choose to walk in the paths of the enemy, or simply ignore the call that God has on our lives, then we are using our free will to open a door for Satan to have authority over our destiny. For example, Proverbs 6:22-23 tells us that those who go down to the house of the adulteress (or adulterer) are treading a pathway that leads to death. And in Psalm 91 we read that it is those who dwell in the shelter of the Most High who are under His protection, for He becomes their 'refuge and fortress'.

I passionately believe that when we live in the holy fear of the living God and walk in His ways, then we are denying the enemy the opportunity to shorten our days through the law of sowing and reaping being applied in our lives (Galatians 6:7-8). None of us can determine just how many our days shall be, but it is good to know we can extend them by taking seriously the scriptural encouragement to live godly lives. A God-fearing people truly is a blessed people!

Prayer: *Help me, Lord, to always make godly choices in my life so that my days will be extended and the enemy will not be able to use my sinfulness to undermine the work of God in my life. In Jesus' name, Amen.*

Personal Notes

_____

_____

_____

_____

_____

Day 7

Obeying God

'I will always obey your law, for ever and ever. I will walk about in freedom, for I have sought your precepts. I will speak of your statutes before kings and will not be put to shame, for I delight in your commands because I love them.' Psalm 119:44-47

For thirty years and more I have watched as people have come through the doors of Ellel centres around the world on their way to Healing Retreats, Training Courses or Conferences. It doesn't matter which country you are in, or which people group they come from, when you look at their faces you can so often see that they have been on a tough journey through life. Some of the battle scars they have picked up along the way are evident! It is sometimes clear that, for various reasons, they haven't been walking about in freedom.

The whole of Psalm 119 is about the laws and the precepts of God – about how precious they are and that, when we follow them, they give us wisdom beyond the intellect of man. In these remarkable verses, from this the longest Psalm, the psalmist expresses a core truth that lies at the heart of much of the healing that people receive. When they come in humility and submit their lives to the scrutiny of the Spirit of God, letting His Word and His truth be the arbiter of what has been right or wrong in their lives, healing will follow.

Pride would want us to adjust the implications of Scripture to make it look as though we are never wrong. Humility recognises that in our heart there is a constant vulnerability to temptation and that when we succumb to it, we sin – and the fact is, sin has consequences. We cannot walk about in freedom when we have been bound by the consequences of our own ungodly choices – choices which are contrary to the laws and precepts of God.

No wonder the psalmist came to the conclusion that there is nothing more sensible than to delight in obeying God's law. When we live within the limits of these provisions of God's mercy, then the enemy has no rights or grounds to enslave us in bondage – we are free!

To walk about in such freedom is a totally liberating experience which brings a smile to our faces, a spring to our step and rejoicing in the heart. Nothing gives me more joy than to see the changes in people's faces when they begin to walk about in the freedom that confession, forgiveness, deliverance and healing always brings. No wonder Isaiah prophesied that the Sovereign Lord was coming to set the captives free! (Isaiah 61:1).

In Psalm 19:7-8, David put it this way: 'The law of the LORD is perfect, reviving the soul. The statutes of the LORD are trustworthy, making wise the simple. The precepts of the LORD are right, giving joy to the heart. The commands of the LORD are radiant, giving light to the eyes.' What incredible fruit from obeying God's law – revival, wisdom, joy and His radiant light in our eyes!

Prayer: Thank You, Lord, that in Your Word You have given us the keys of salvation and that when I choose to walk in Your ways, then I will always know the freedom that only You can give. Help me, Lord, to remember Your laws and rejoice to walk in them forever and ever! In the name of Jesus, Amen.

Personal Notes

Day 8

Are You Lost?

'Thomas said to him, "Lord, we don't know where you are going, so how can we know the way?" Jesus answered, "I am the way and the truth and the life. No-one comes to the Father except through me."' John 14:5-6

Sometimes life is a bit like an unknown jungle or a maze! In the jungle, there are tall trees rising up out of heavy undergrowth, interspersed with many different tracks and pathways and, apparently, no signposts. I once watched a film about a boy who was lost in the forests of the Pacific North West. Whichever way he looked, all the pathways through the forest looked the same – there was no indication whatsoever as to which was the way out. From ground level the jungle is an impossible barrier to escape from.

In many of our old English country houses, the gardeners would build a maze of thick, high hedges, for the entertainment of the family and visitors. The more complicated the maze the harder it was to get to the seat where you could rest in the middle. But once in, there is only one way out and it's easy to get trapped.

If you are high up, however, you can look down on the jungle or the maze, and see at a glance which is the right way to go to get out of the mess you're in. And if you're on the ground and have a mobile phone, the person who is high up, looking down on you, can easily direct your steps, so that you know exactly which direction to go at any time.

Long before man invented the mobile phone, God showed man how He could speak directly into the hearts of His children. He didn't need a phone, but we did need to have the ears of our spirit open to listen in to the communication channel we call prayer. He is high and lifted up (Isaiah 6:1) and from His vantage point He can see everything that's happening. No matter how thick the jungles of life may be or how complicated the maze, we don't need to be lost.

Jesus expressed this wonderful truth so simply and powerfully, when He said to Thomas "'I am the way!'" It's not a pathway we need to follow – it's a Person – a Person who can see the way ahead and who longs to speak to His children and give them the benefit of His wisdom and direction. He has promised that He will show us His way for our lives. One of the songs we used to sing at our church youth group was:

'My Lord, knows the way through the wilderness,
All I have to do is follow!'
(Sidney Edward Cox)

The words may be simple, but they are incredibly profound. Following Him requires us to humble ourselves, submit to His authority in our lives and walk in obedience – and then we will find our way out of the jungles or the mazes of life. And once having found our way out of whatever mess we have been in, we can then listen to His voice of encouragement and direction. The best decisions I have ever made have been ones that were definitely what God was telling me to do. And the worst were those when I thought I knew best. I soon learnt that God's way is preferable – every time!

Prayer: *Thank You, Lord, that You have promised to show me the way. Help me to have my ears always open to listen to Your voice so that I can know where to put my feet on my journey through life. In Jesus' name, Amen.*

Personal Notes

Day 9

The Sacrifice of Fools

'Guard your steps when you go to the house of GOD. Go near to listen rather than to offer the sacrifice of fools, who do not know that they do wrong.' Ecclesiastes 5:1

Many years ago, I underlined those three words, 'sacrifice of fools', in my Bible and thought that one day I would write a book with that title. Well, the years have passed and the book remains unwritten, but the profound principle represented by these three words seems more relevant than ever in today's world – especially in a formerly very Christian country such as the United Kingdom.

For, as time has passed, we have seen more and more of the foundational scriptural principles that used to be at the heart of government eliminated from our statute books and removed from the educational curricula of our children. The UK is not alone in this – many, if not most, countries have taken a similar path. God, and the principles spelled out in His Word, have become an embarrassment to a nation that is now almost exclusively secular.

But it's even more sad when believers in God absorb the world's views, visit church and offer their worship, but at the same time are not willing to listen to what God has said in His Word. To say that you love Jesus but refuse to live your life in willing obedience to what He taught, is a prime example of the hypocrisy which made Jesus so angry with the Pharisees. It is simply the sacrifice of fools.

People have absorbed a Gospel of Salvation, which they largely interpret as meaning 'when I die, I'll go to Heaven'. But they forget that Jesus didn't come to proclaim a Gospel of Salvation, he began his ministry by preaching the good news (meaning the Gospel) of the Kingdom, which has a very different meaning. For when we come to faith in Jesus we become citizens of a new kingdom, and as citizens we are (or should be) under the authority of the King. That means living according to the ways of God and not the ways of the world. So the Gospel of the Kingdom has a radical effect on the way we live here on earth and is not a spiritual insurance policy for what happens when we die.

The King delights to guide and direct the subjects of His Kingdom. We cannot expect to hear His voice leading us on through life if what we bring to him in worship is the sacrifice of fools. We read in Proverbs 8:32 and 8:34 that those who are blessed are the ones who listen to the Lord and those who live their lives according to God's ways.

Today, one of the most offensive words in the English language is 'sin'. No-one wants to know that there is a God who sees and that there is a consequence to breaking His laws. But as David said in Psalm 14:1, 'The fool says in his heart, "There is no GOD"'. It's foolish to ignore God and effectively tell Him that you're going to live life your way. Sin is a very dangerous disease. And Paul spelled it out very clearly in Romans 6:23 when he said 'the wages of sin is death'!

So, may I urge you not to offer God 'the sacrifice of fools', but to humble yourself before Him, choose to listen to what He says and walk in His ways, rather than close your ears to His voice and your eyes to His Word.

Prayer: *I am sorry, Lord, for those times that, in hypocrisy, I have offered You the sacrifice of fools – worshipped You with my lips but walked away from You in my heart. Please forgive me, Lord, for the times I have done this and help me to offer You a sacrifice of real praise whenever I come before You. In Jesus' name, Amen.*

Personal Notes

Day 10

The Walk of Faith

'"Brothers, choose seven men from among you who are known to be full of the Spirit and wisdom. We will turn this responsibility over to them and will give our attention to prayer and the ministry of the word." The proposal pleased the whole group. They chose Stephen, a man full of faith and the Holy Spirit and …' Acts 6:3-5

Faith is the ability to not just believe in the existence of God, but also to recognise the voice of the One in whom you have believed and, when He shows you the way to go, take action and follow Him.

Hebrews 11 lists a veritable catalogue of men and women whose faith led them to do mighty acts for the Lord. They weren't the sort of people who sat in their armchair 'full of faith' but then did nothing! They were men and women of action as well as faith. A person who is full of faith is under the authority of their commanding officer (Jesus) and gladly obeys Him. Indeed, Hebrews 11:7 tells us that it was 'in holy fear' that Noah exercised his faith and built the ark. He had no intention of failing in his obedience!

Stephen was one of the seven men who were chosen to act as administrators in the developing church fellowship. Even though his role was administrative, it was still essential for him to be full of the Spirit and wisdom – the primary requisites of anyone who is given permission to exercise responsibility over others in the church. Without the Spirit they would be operating in the flesh, doing what seemed to be good to them alone and not what seemed good to the Holy Spirit also. When the motives of the heart are not in line with the purposes of God it's very easy to make big mistakes – both in your personal life and in the leadership of others.

The Holy Spirit gave Stephen the necessary wisdom and he exercised his faith with courage. He was not afraid to use his gifting and power, and God did 'great wonders and miraculous signs among the people' (Acts 6:8) through him.

It is this linking of wisdom with Holy Spirit empowering that equips us to make godly choices at each stage of our life. And it acts as powerful encouragement when we are stepping out in the right direction. This is how God has always led and directed His people – and it is how He will direct your steps as well. It also acts as a warning bell when, in our humanity, we might want to do something that is not God's best plan for our lives.

When faced with decisions that have to be made, we can then look at all the circumstances carefully, pray and look to the Lord for Him to guide us by His Holy Spirit, revealing the direction He would want us to go. And when we have tested our decision, sometimes with those who would also pray in a similar way, we can move forward with faith and in confidence that God is with us, even if, as in Stephen's case, we have to face tough and even threatening circumstances.

Because of his faith Stephen was picked out for close attention by the religious authorities – watched closely by a young man called Saul – and he became the first Christian martyr. Throughout history there have been many believers who have died for their faith. And today, we are hearing of more and more believers in various parts of the world who are once again facing the reality of becoming martyrs. So, alongside our desire to receive God's guidance we should also pray for His courage so that we will be able to follow Him faithfully all our days, come what may.

Prayer: *Thank You for showing me how Stephen was selected to serve you with a special responsibility in the Church. Help me, Lord to look to You for both wisdom and Holy Spirit empowering to help me in all the decisions I have to make through life. And give me the courage to be faithful in my obedience as I follow You. In Jesus' name, Amen.*

Personal Notes

Day 11

Are You Ready?

'So, Joshua ordered the officers of the people: "Go through the camp and tell the people, 'Get your supplies ready. Three days from now you will cross the Jordan here to go in and take possession of the land the LORD *your God is giving you for your own.'"'* Joshua 1:10-11

Joshua was given a big job! He had to stand in the shoes of Moses as leader of the people and take them forward into the land that God had promised them so long ago. The time had now come to step forward in faith, notwithstanding his own misgivings. God had spoken and told him, *'"Be strong and courageous. Do not be terrified; do not be discouraged, for the* LORD *your God will be with you wherever you go"'* (Joshua 1:9). He was ready – even if apprehensive and nervous.

This message now had to be relayed to the people so that that they could get ready to move. The officers went through the camp telling them to be ready, for in three days' time they were going to cross the River Jordan and enter the land that God was giving them as their own. There must have been a huge sense of anticipation, excitement and, yes, fear as they wondered what would happen next when God's historic promises to Israel began to be fulfilled.

But God wasn't going to do it for them. They had to put their own feet down on the ground, one step at a time and move! God didn't send a chariot of fire to lift them off the ground and drop them by angelic parachute into the land of promise! They had to move their own feet forward in faith before God would do the miraculous on their behalf. When they came to the river it was only as the priests put their feet in the waters of the river, which was in flood, that God worked the miracle. God didn't stop the river's flow and then say "It's now OK to go." He required the people to move forward in faith and as they did so they realised that God was clearing the way for them.

I have met a number of people over the years whom God had called to serve Him. But they were waiting for God to do the miraculous and lift them supernaturally out of their present situation and land them in the place of promise. Sadly many years later they were still waiting for their miracle – and it never came.

When God shows us His plan for our lives He expects us to get ready and start moving forward in faith, preparing ourselves for whatever He has asked us to do. God can then direct our steps as we go. Just as a car has to be moving before the steering wheel can be turned, we have to start moving forward in faith, so that God can then direct our steps.

So, may I encourage you to look at the land of your life that lies before you and get yourself ready to start moving! Just as Joshua gave the people three days to prepare themselves, take time to review all that God has already spoken into your life and look to Him for His leading for the days ahead as you step into His plans and purposes.

Prayer: *Thank You, Lord, for Your hand on my life down the years and now, at this present time, help me to step forward in faith into all that You have planned for me. Thank you for the promise to Joshua that You would be with him and for the encouragement those words are as I step out in faith into the destiny You have prepared for me. In Jesus' name, Amen.*

Personal Notes

_____

_____

_____

_____

_____

_____

_____

_____

_____

_____

_____

Day 12

The Five Keys of Successful Living

'Be on your guard; stand firm in the faith; be men of courage; be strong. Do everything in love.' 1 Corinthians 16:13

In this scripture Paul hands us a keyring from which five keys are hanging. They are keys which have been given to us by the Lord to use on our journey of faith. They are keys to successful living – not success as measured by the very materialistic world in which we are living, but success as seen from the perspectives of the spiritual realms and eternity.

Paul was a great teacher. He had the wonderful gift of being able to encapsulate profound principles in just a few words. If followed these principles will enable believers to not just live out their days on planet earth, but to live them well, in harmony with our Creator and in anticipation of enjoying eternity in fellowship with Him and with other believers.

The first key, '**be on your guard'**, helps us to recognise that we are living in a world where Satan has been given authority (by man) as the god of this world. Satan's strategy is to use temptation as a means of distracting us on our journey so that we then step off the way that God has laid before us. It's not surprising, therefore, that Paul warns us to be on our guard against everything that the enemy can throw at us to try and take us off course. In Ephesians 6:10-18 Paul gives us detailed instructions about how to use the armour of God in the fight of faith.

Secondly he urges us to **stand firm in the faith** – that means stand firm in what we know to be the truth from the Word of God. In 1 Timothy 4:16 Paul tells Timothy to 'watch [his] life and doctrine closely'. Paul knew that if we get off course and finish up in deception the consequences for us as believers are serious. We are in danger of missing all that God has prepared for us here on earth and, even more seriously, of losing our reward in eternity.

The third and fourth keys urge us to **be courageous** and to **be strong** – in much the same way as God urged Joshua as he led the children of Israel into their Promised Land, *'Be strong and courageous. Do not be afraid or terrified … for the* LORD *your God goes with you; he will never leave your nor forsake you'* (Deuteronomy 31:6). Courage and strength are not just qualities of big people with physical prowess. They are the characteristic of all those who run their race of life, intent on achieving their goal (Philippians 3:12).

The final key reinforces the message of the wonderful Chapter 13 of 1 Corinthians. We must **do everything in love**, for without love in our hearts even the good things we do are of little value. It was love that took Jesus to the cross and He tells us to take up our cross and follow Him.

So, as you press on to make a success of everything you do for the rest of your days, keep this keyring in your spiritual pocket – and never forget to use the keys on a daily basis!

Prayer: *Thank You, Lord, for these wonderful keys to living the Christian life. Help me, Lord, to always remember that they are intended for daily use and I pray that You will strengthen me day by day with Your Holy Spirit to live for You. In the name of Jesus, Amen.*

Personal Notes

Day 13

Test, Hold On and Avoid!

'Test everything, hold on to the good. Avoid every kind of evil.' 1 Thessalonians 5:21

Many of the mistakes that people make in their decisions about life come from failing to heed Paul's advice to the Thessalonians. In reality, it wasn't just good advice, it was a command – an essential instruction to help believers make good and God-honouring decisions.

We are commanded to be sure to test all things so we can avoid the dangers of deception. If we fail to test things we could be in danger of being deceived. And one of the commonest deceptions is to think that it's OK for us to re-interpret the Word of God to make it mean whatever we want it to mean!

The last part of our scripture simply tells us to avoid every kind of evil – for Paul knew that if we fall into the practice of sin then God's Spirit within us will be quenched and it will affect our relationship with Him. Proverbs 3:7-8 puts it even more strongly. Here it says *'Do not be wise in your own eyes; fear the LORD and avoid evil. This will bring health to your body and nourishment to your bones.'* From this we understand that there can even be a direct relationship between the way we live and our physical health!

If we truly have a holy fear of a holy God, then we will not want to live our lives outside the provisions of God's Word. He has given us the Scriptures so that we will know the truth – and then, when we obey the truth, Jesus said, *'the truth will set you free'* (John 8:32).

So when it comes to testing things, the first place we should go to check whether or not something is of God is the Word of God. If we find that what we are thinking about or doing, is contrary to Scripture, then we can be sure it has failed the test. We can hold on to those things that are good and are of God but, if it is clear from God's Word that something is not of Him and is therefore sinful, then the instruction is clear (in both Paul's teaching and the Proverbs), we should avoid it!

If we come to God asking Him to guide and direct our steps through life while at the same time choosing to do things that are contrary to the teaching of God's Word, then we can't expect to be able to hear His voice in our hearts. In Psalm 66:18 the psalmist tells us *'if I had cherished sin in my heart, the LORD would not have listened.'*

It is strikingly clear therefore that if we fail to test things in the way God has told us to, then we put ourselves at risk. Similar considerations need to be applied to a 'word from the Lord' that someone may have given you. Are you sure it was for you? Have you tested both the content against God's Word and its relevance to you and your life's circumstances? If not, then you might be choosing to follow someone else's nice idea, rather than the pathway that God has chosen for you. To test something is not to doubt God, but to trust that He will make His will clear for you.

Prayer: *I'm sorry, Lord, for those times when I have not tested things and as a result have chosen to do things that are contrary to Your will, Your Word and Your plan for my life. I pray that You will forgive me for the mistakes I have made and cleanse me from the consequences. Help me, Lord, to remember to test things carefully against Your Word so that I can hold on to what is good and avoid what is bad. In Jesus' name, Amen.*

Personal Notes

Day 14

I was About to Fall, but God ... !

*'I was pushed back and about to fall, but the L*ORD *helped me. The* L*ORD *is my strength and my song; he has become my salvation.'*
Psalm 118:13-14

Many are the times when God's people have been in a situation where only God could help them – times when circumstances prevailed against them, especially when their enemies attacked and it looked as though they were heading for certain defeat; times like when Moses was facing the Red Sea and the Egyptian armies were rapidly gaining ground and there was no way of escape. These are the times when our cries for God to guide us reach desperation point!

In this psalm, the psalmist remembers many such times when he was beyond human help and knew that, were it not for God's intervention, he would have been overwhelmed and overcome. He would have fallen and been defeated.

There are times in all our lives when God allows us to get into a situation which is beyond our human capacity to fix it. We have done everything we can, but there seems no way forward - no way out of the mess. The pressures are more than we can stand. Here, the psalmist remembers how *'all the nations surrounded'* him; how they *'swarmed like bees'* around him and he was *'pushed back and about to fall.'*

Then he says, *'But the* LORD *...'* Time and again when he was in this sort of situation he had learned that there is only one thing to do – and that is trust God and later have yet another reason to proclaim that *'the* LORD *helped me ... The* LORD'*s right hand has done mighty things!'*

There are many times in the history of Ellel Ministries when God has intervened in dire situations, when there was absolutely nothing we could do. On occasions we were swamped with the desperate needs of those who had come for help and who were struggling with major issues that we had never seen before and didn't understand. At other times we were desperate for funds to pay the bills of the ministry and push forward with the plans that God had clearly laid before us.

And then there were times when we were just totally exhausted and ready to drop, but in circumstances where it was impossible not to carry on and push through! Our testimony is that God heard our cry, intervened and the work continued to grow and be blessed.

In 2 Corinthians 8:12-20 Paul describes a catalogue of really serious things that he had had to face across the years of his ministry, but the Lord had helped him!

If you are struggling right now, for whatever reason, may I encourage you to stop whatever else you are doing and read the whole of Psalm 118 out loud. Proclaim the blessings of the Lord who heard and answered the cries of His people. And then spend a few minutes recounting with thanksgiving the times in your own life when God intervened. Praise encourages the spirit and lifts the soul. And then, in the words that conclude the psalm, *'Give thanks to the LORD, for he is good; his love endures for ever.'*

Prayer: *My heart is full of gratitude to You, Lord, for Your love and Your faithfulness. Thank You for the ways Your hand does mighty things for Your people. Help me, Lord, to trust You even more when all around seems to be falling apart, knowing that You are able to do over and above anything that I can ever think or dream of! Thank You, Lord. Amen.*

Personal Notes

Day 15

God's Unchangeable Laws

'Do not be deceived. God cannot be mocked. A man reaps what he sows. The one who sows to please his sinful nature, from that nature will reap destruction; the one who sows to please the Spirit, from the Spirit will reap eternal life. Let us not become weary in doing good, for at the proper time we will reap a harvest, if we do not give up.' Galatians 6:7-9

When we sow from a packet of bean seeds, we are not surprised when beans begin to sprout from the ground and in due course we are able to pick the harvest. Equally, when we plant seeds of forget-me-nots, we are not surprised that before long we can enjoy the delicate blue spring flowers in our garden. This is the natural law of God's order which is divinely written into the whole of God's creation. What you reap is always a consequence of what you sow.

In exactly the same way Paul is telling us, through this scripture, that the nature of the seed we sow in our lives will also be evident from its consequences. He says that if we sow to satisfy the base desires of our carnal nature we will, in due time, inherit death. But if we sow to please the Holy Spirit, then the ultimate fruit is eternal life. What an extraordinary contrast between the two crops – death and life!

Throughout Scripture we read the same fundamental message. Paul put it this way in his letter to the Romans, *'For the wages of sin is death, but the gift of God is eternal life in Christ Jesus our Lord'* (Romans 6:23). It is a message that the world does not want to hear – self-indulgence and the enjoyment of sin are considered to be the meat and drink of a godless generation. But our scripture says that God is not mocked and that good fruit will not come from bad seed.

So how should we respond when we suddenly realise that we have wasted time and character on a lifestyle which has left behind the scars of sin and there is now bad fruit in our lives? The past cannot be undone, but, thanks be to God, true repentance is always followed by true forgiveness. However, we may still bear the scars of the past, which need healing, even though the slate is wiped clean for eternity when God fulfils his promise, which says *'"Come now, let us settle the matter," says the LORD. "Though your sins are like scarlet, they shall be as white as snow; though they are red as crimson, they shall be like wool"'* (Isaiah 1:18).

Many is the time I have wept with those who are weeping over their wasted years – but I have also been thrilled to rejoice with those who rejoice when forgiveness comes and a fresh start is made, this time sowing good seed – seed which pleases the Holy Spirit and produces good fruit.

The fruit of the Holy Spirit's influence in our lives is neatly summarised for us in Galatians 5:22-23: love, joy, peace, patience, kindness, goodness, faithfulness, gentleness and self-control. As Paul so rightly then says, there is no law against such things. No law of God is broken by them and there are no negative consequences.

Prayer: Help me, Lord, to always remember that whatever I sow in my life will have consequences. Forgive me, Lord, for those times when I have knowingly sown bad seed – but thank You so much for Your forgiveness. I pray that You will guide me from now on as I choose to walk in step with the Your Holy Spirit and do those things that please Him. In Jesus' name, Amen.

Personal Notes

_____

_____

_____

_____

_____

_____

_____

_____

_____

_____

Day 16

Known by God

'O LORD, you have searched me and you know me. You know when I sit and when I rise; you perceive my thoughts from afar. You discern my going out and my lying down; you are familiar with all my ways.' Psalm 139:1-3

There are few places we can go these days, whether in a big city, travelling by train, bus or plane, or almost anywhere people gather, without some sort of surveillance camera catching our every movement. Even in the small market town where we live there are hidden cameras, recording what the local people are doing, all in the name of security.

In today's environment we almost take such observation cameras for granted as being necessary for our safety. We are relieved when they are used to record some criminal activity and catch the culprit. No-one is really interested in what the majority of us are doing, but when something bad happens the police are very interested to see if surveillance cameras have recorded the incident.

On a much wider front, whenever there's an international sporting festival such as the Olympic Games, or a major incident occurs anywhere in the world, it can all be screened instantly by TV into the living rooms of people all over the planet!

If, with man's very limited knowledge and ability, these amazing things are possible, it should be no surprise that the all-knowing God is also able to watch over every detail of our lives and know everything that has ever happened to us from conception to the present day. He doesn't need security cameras to keep an eye on us!

This is something that David, the psalmist, knew instinctively. In Psalm 139 he recognises that, if there is nowhere he can go to escape from the presence of God (vs 7-12), then there is absolutely nothing that God doesn't know about everything he has done and will do – the good and the not-so-good. And there is absolutely no circumstance or place that any of us can be in where we cannot cry out to God for His help and guidance.

David imagines being able to fly on the wings of the dawn and settle on the far side of the sea and declares *'even there your hand will guide me, your right hand will hold me fast'* (v 10). He didn't think it would ever be possible to walk on the moon, but when James Irwin, the Apollo 15 astronaut, turned to prayer when he had a problem on the surface of the moon, he had an extraordinary encounter with the living God who heard and answered his prayer. He came back to earth a changed man and devoted the rest of his days to sharing the truth that Jesus really is the way, the truth and the life (John 14:6). Wherever you are in God's great universe, God is there with you.

I discovered in my business years that God is the best businessman I have ever known! The supernatural 'coincidences' and the ideas that could only have come from God were always the most successful and profitable developments. I learnt to trust the ideas that bore the hallmark of God's Holy Spirit and was never disappointed.

So, never think that your situation or problem are beyond the knowledge and wisdom of God or beyond Him being able to provide a solution. He can and will hold you fast and show you the way to go.

Prayer: *Thank You, Lord, for these wonderful words from Scripture. I know that I can trust You to lead and direct my steps wherever I am. I pray that You will help me to overcome the problems I have to face today as I listen to Your voice and watch for Your leading. In Jesus' name, Amen.*

Personal Notes

Day 17

See If ...

'Search me, O God, and know my heart, test me and know my anxious thoughts. See if there be any offensive way in me; and lead me in the way everlasting.' Psalm 139:23-24

In yesterday's devotional we saw how David, the psalmist, recognised that there is nowhere we can go to escape the presence of God. As a result, we can know also that there is absolutely nothing that God doesn't know about our lives from the moment of conception till the present day. Even though our first thought might be "Oh no!", in reality it is wonderfully good news that God knows the very worst there can possibly be about us and His arms of love are still wide open for each one of us.

David, of course, had first-hand experience of God knowing what he had done. Even though he had desperately tried to cover up his sin of adultery with Bathsheba and then arranged for the death of Bathsheba's husband, Uriah, God had seen what had happened. In 2 Samuel 11 we read how God told Nathan, the prophet, to go and confront David about his sin. It must have been a devastating moment for David to realise that nothing of what he had done was hidden from God.

But as you read more in the Scriptures about David's life, you soon realise that the sins of his past did not define his future. God still loved him and we read in Psalm 51 about David's journey of healing and restoration. But God knew that unless the past was exposed and healed, David would always be on the defensive, trying to hide something sinful he was ashamed of. Bringing it into the light so he could look at himself in the 'mirror of life' was absolutely essential for David's future calling and destiny.

Indeed, this daily process of looking to God for direction became so important for David that he came to God with the prayer which is our scripture for today. *'Search me LORD, know my heart, test me and see if there is anything in me that offends You.'* The King James version of the Bible is even more blunt: *'see if there be any wicked way in me, and lead me in the way everlasting.'*

This is the prayer of humility which releases the healing and the power of God into our lives. The relief which flows through a person's spirit when everything is laid open on the table before God, is like the waters of a river that have been blocked by a dam suddenly breaking out, washing away all the debris and leaving everything clean again.

Truly knowing that you are still loved in such circumstances is one of the most healing experiences anyone can ever know. Not only does it release the past, but it clears the channels so that you can once again hear God for yourself with a clean heart, trusting that He will indeed continue to lead you in the way everlasting. This is the joy that comes from healing through forgiveness!

Prayer: *Thank You, Lord, that there is nothing about me that You don't already know and that You still love me. I ask You, Lord, to truly show me myself as I look into Your mirror so that I can put right all that You show me is wrong. Thank You for Your continued leading and direction in my life. In Jesus' name, Amen.*

Personal Notes

Day 18

Action Words

'The people who do know their God will be strong and do exploits.' Daniel 11:32 (KJV)

There are three key phrases in our scripture for today: *'know their God'*, *'will be strong'* and *'do exploits'*. These are the action words which draw us into supernatural involvement with Father God. There is a divine logic about this sequence which teaches us a profound lesson about both the protocol of God and the way He guides people into their destiny.

First we have to **know Him**, and that doesn't just mean know who He is, but really get to know Him. It means to be in a close relationship with Him, to understand His heart, recognise His voice and be happy to walk in His ways. Unless we have come to that place, we will not know what it is that God is calling us to be or to do. The more we read Scripture, the more we will grow to understand and know His character. And the more we pray the message of Scripture into our spirit, the more the truth of Scripture will become a lens through which we can see God, as well as a mirror in which we can see ourselves.

Once you know Him like this, it will be easier for you to discern what God is calling you to do as you follow Him. So, there is no need to fear or doubt about the future for He is utterly trustworthy. He will lead you one step at a time. And when you have reached that place of being confident in Him, you will then **be strong** – in fact so strong that nothing will be able to stand in the way of His purposes being fulfilled.

The result will be that you will then begin to **do exploits** – amazing things that only God could have prepared in advance for you to do, as Paul expressed it in his letter to the Ephesians (2:10).

In the history of Christian missions, we read many stories about men and women who knew God like this, heard His voice calling them and then pioneered major new doorways for the Christian message to be taken through. Many had extraordinary adventures with God as they took the Gospel to the farthest corners of the earth.

Take a few minutes to look up people like Hudson Taylor (of China), Mary Slessor (of Calabar), C T Studd (of China, India and Central Africa), Wilfrid Grenfell (of Labrador) and hundreds more whose faith and obedience has had the effect of transforming the lives of millions of believers who came to faith as a result of their endeavours.

If I'm ever going through a difficult time I choose to read such biographies. It is hugely encouraging to read how God was with them through their own difficult experiences and to learn life-changing lessons from the way they learned to trust God in the face of seeming impossibilities and do such amazing exploits for the Kingdom of God!

I pray that as you seek to know Him better, you will get excited at the prospect of doing exploits for Him. Then, one day, you will look back at the journey you have been on and be amazed at what God has done.

Prayer: *Thank You, Lord, that You are still in the business of calling people like Daniel to be strong and do exploits for the Kingdom of God. Help me to keep my eyes always open to see what You are doing and my ears always alert to listen to what You are saying, so that I will know what it is that You want me to do next for You. In Jesus' name, Amen.*

Personal Notes

Day 19

What Do These Stones Mean?

'Each of you is to take up a stone on his shoulder, according to the number of the tribes of the Israelites, to serve as a sign among you in the future. When your children ask you "What do these stones mean?", tell them that the flow of the Jordan was cut off before the ark of the covenant of the LORD. When it crossed the Jordan the waters of the Jordan were cut off. These stones are to be a memorial to the people of Israel forever.' Joshua 4:5-7

When God does something special it needs to be recorded and remembered. The testimony of what God has done in the past is a reminder to the generations yet to come of the reality of who God is and of His faithfulness to one generation after another. I recently re-read the book *Missionary Warrior: Charles E Cowman*. It is the extraordinary story of how one young man determined to trust God – and God alone – for his provision and supply when establishing missions in Japan in the earliest years of the twentieth century.

The book is written by his wife, Lettie Cowman, who faithfully recorded miracle after miracle that God did in response to their daily obedience to the vision they had been given. Every chapter is filled with 'piles of memorial stones' as she not only shares personal testimony to God's provision but expresses amazing gems of Christian truth that could only have been learned on the sharp end of trust and obedience to God.

As a result of all their experiences of God's faithfulness, Mrs Cowman wrote *Streams in the Desert,* which for nearly a hundred years now has been one of the most loved, valued and blessed books of daily devotional readings. What she wrote was not just the clever words of a good writer, but the living expression of what had been burnt into her heart.

I will always be grateful for my own parents who regularly told us with enthusiasm and excitement of the things that God had done in their lives. As I grew up I had no reason to doubt the reality of who God is, because I was soaked in the living testimony of day-to-day Christian reality. Mum and Dad were regularly adding 'stones' to the pile of memories that would stand me in good stead throughout my life – and even today they have the capacity to freshly impact and challenge my own faith and walk with the Lord.

So, may I encourage you to write down the things that God has done in your life and regularly look at this 'pile of precious stones', reminding yourself of the goodness of God and His faithfulness – and don't hesitate to tell the next generation what God has done. The stories I was told have been an encouragement to me for the whole of my life and I have often re-told them in my teaching ministry.

This is exactly what Psalm 105 and Hebrews 11 are all about – they are both a catalogue of the Lord's goodness and faithfulness to His people. Be blessed as you read these chapters for yourself and be encouraged that the God of the psalmist and of the writer of Hebrews is the same God who sent His Son to redeem you out of the hand of the enemy. What a faithful God we serve!

Prayer: Thank You, Lord, for all the evidences of Your faithfulness there have been in my life. Help me to take time to remember what You have done and let these things be an encouragement and a challenge to keep being faithful to You for the rest of my days. In Jesus' name, Amen.

Personal Notes

_____

_____

_____

_____

_____

_____

_____

_____

Day 20

'Should Have Gone to Specsavers!'

'Jesus told them this parable: "Can a blind man lead a blind man? Will they not both fall into a pit? A student is not above his teacher, but everyone who is fully trained will be like his teacher."' Luke 6:39

In our scripture for today God warns against being led by a blind man into a pit. How important it is to check out the spiritual sight of those who lead us! There is a popular series of advertisements on British television from a firm of opticians which shows people making huge, and sometimes very funny, mistakes because their eyesight was defective. The adverts always end with the words 'Should have gone to Specsavers!'

The plumb-line of truth in the scriptures is God's spiritual equivalent to Specsavers, the opticians. It's important that we all have our spiritual eyesight tested against God's Word. But the mistakes we can make when we don't and can't 'see' properly are not funny, they can be of eternal consequence. None of us want to hear the equivalent of words such as these spoken over our own life at the end of time – 'Should have gone to Specsavers!'

It is a fact that students learn from and grow to be like their teachers. What their teachers teach is information which becomes a foundation of their pupils' lives. For that reason Christian teachers are especially accountable before the Lord for ensuring that what they teach is faithful to God's Word and they need to check their spiritual eyesight regularly!

When Paul was training Timothy to be an apostolic leader, he told him, *'Watch your life and your doctrine closely. Persevere in them, because if you do, you will save both yourself and your hearers'* (1 Timothy 4:16). Paul was making it clear that good teaching would save Timothy's hearers, but implies that bad teaching (from blind teachers) would lead them astray.

So back to the blind man. If a leader is blind to God's truth and is going astray, then that leader's blindness will become the blindness of those who hear and follow. If someone is teaching false doctrine, then those who hear are in danger, because they are likely to believe the same false doctrine that their teacher is teaching. It is absolutely vital, therefore, that we learn how to use the gift of discernment. Through this the Holy Spirit can warn us of beliefs that are wrong and of spiritual pits that we are in danger of being led into.

73

In these very testing days, when there are so many unscriptural beliefs gaining ground and influence inside various sectors of the church, we need to be very much on our guard – for things may be being taught that are not true to the Word of God. We need to look carefully at what the Word of God says, so that we will have a true plumb line against which to measure whether or not what we are being taught and what we believe is faithful to God's truth or otherwise.

These are the days that Jesus warned us about twice in Matthew 24 – especially the danger of being led astray by false prophets. We must be careful of people who preface their words with "Thus says the Lord", when it isn't the Lord who has spoken. Jeremiah also warned of this danger. Through him, God said: *'I did not send these prophets, yet they have run with their message; I did not speak to them, yet they have prophesied'* (Jeremiah 23:21).

We need to be sure that our spiritual sight is true and tested if we are to avoid making serious mistakes which can, sometimes, have life-long consequences.

Prayer: *Thank You, Lord, for warning me against being led astray by blind leaders. Help me to discern truth from error in my own life and to regularly check out my spiritual eyesight against the sight chart of God's Word. In Jesus' name. Amen.*

Personal Notes

Day 21

God Has Unshakeable Plans

'Then Job replied to the Lord, "I know that you can do all things; no plan of yours can be thwarted."' Job 42:1-2

It's easy sometimes to look at all that's going on in the world and wonder if God has noticed how desperate things are. Can't you see, Lord, how man is continually violating Your Word and perverting Your laws? Can't You see, Lord, how people who do not know You are using their power and authority to do terrible things all over the earth? Don't you know, Lord, that people are calling good evil and evil good? Haven't you noticed, Lord, that Your enemies are gaining ground?

But as with all things in God, there is another side to the story and a timing in history that is critical to the plans of God. We saw with the birth of Jesus that there was a right time for Him to come and fulfil the prophecies of Isaiah and other prophets. And, as the Psalmist expresses it, *'The wicked plot against the righteous and gnash their teeth at them; but the LORD laughs at the wicked, for he knows their day is coming'* (Psalm 37:12-13).

And so it is today – the world may have chosen to reject the authority of God's Word and become their own authority, but just as the law of gravity is unchangeable, so are God's laws. And one day, again when the time is right, God has made it very clear that there is a time coming when the wicked will regret their scoffing at the authority of God. While there may be many things yet to unfold, no-one can deny that world events are happening at a frightening speed.

The earth is groaning with pain and those who love the Lord are desperate for the joy that will come in the morning, when our Saviour bursts through the clouds at the right time. Let us never forget that God has had a plan from the very beginning. Two thousand years ago Part One of His redemptive plan was fulfilled. Part Two cannot be very far away!

No matter what Satan and all the powers of darkness might do to pervert and control the world through rebellion and evil, God laughs! His plan cannot be thwarted. Let those who know and love Him be like the wise virgins, ready to welcome Him as the sands of time reach their conclusion and Jesus returns to earth as King of His Kingdom. No wonder both John the Baptist and Jesus began their public ministries by saying *'Repent, for the Kingdom of Heaven is at hand'* (Matthew 4:17). For, as the foolish virgins discovered (Matthew 25:1-10), when He comes it is already too late. God's plans will not be thwarted.

I am reminded of when Jesus said to the disciples *'"Let's go over to the other side of the lake"'* (Luke 8:22). They got into a boat and Jesus promptly fell asleep. Part way across the lake there was a terrible storm and the disciples were in fear that the boat would sink and they cried out, *'"Master, Master, we're going to drown."'* Jesus woke up and calmed the storm, but wanted the disciples to learn from the experience and asked them *'"Where is your faith?"'* Jesus had a purpose in going to the other side of the lake and His purposes were not going to be thwarted by a storm. If He had said they were going to the other side, then that is what they were going to do!

Prayer: *Thank You, Jesus, that You will one day fulfil Part Two of the plans of God and this time the whole world will see Your coming. Thank You that God's plans cannot be thwarted and that nothing which Satan can do will ever frustrate His ultimate plans. Help me to remain faithful to You, until You either take me to yourself or come again! In Jesus' name, Amen.*

Personal Notes

Day 22

The Three Keys of Fruitfulness

'But the seed on good soil stands for those with a noble and good heart, who hear the word, retain it, and by persevering produce a crop.' Luke 8:15

Our scripture for today is the last verse in the parable of the sower. This is, perhaps, one of the most well-known teachings of Jesus, in which He talks about four different types of ground onto which seed is scattered. These are the hard path on which the seed can be trampled underfoot, rocky ground in which it is not possible for the seed to take root, thorny ground in which the seed is choked by the thorns which also grow there and, finally, the good ground in which the seed grows well and produces a good crop.

It is generally assumed that if the seed falls on good ground, it will automatically produce a good crop. But when Jesus applies this teaching to the lives of believers, He expands on what He means by good ground. It is not simply ground that will produce a good crop without any effort. Jesus tells us that there are three keys for ensuring that there really is going to be a good crop arising from the ground of our lives.

The three keys are simple – the first is obvious, **hearing the word.** Unless we actually hear the words that Jesus says we will never be able to apply them in our lives. And I believe that when Jesus is talking about hearing, He is not simply referring to our physical ears hearing a sound, but to the understanding deep in our hearts with the ears of the Spirit, so that what He says becomes real in our lives.

Jesus then says that the seed on good soil also represents those who **retain the word** that has been heard. It is so easy to hear something and even understand it, but then to move on in life and forget it. The things that Jesus said are so important that we need to make every endeavour not only to hear them but also to remember them. If we remember the teaching of Jesus and retain it in our hearts, it will then always be available for us to use and apply in the changing situations of life. For this reason the discipline of reading something from Scripture every day will ensure that we are constantly reminded that God's Word is the source of the truth which guides us in our lives.

The first key is, therefore, *hearing the word;* the second key is *retaining it;* and the third key which Jesus gives us, for ensuring that our lives produce 'a good crop' is **perseverance**. Perseverance implies that there will be a need to press on and through opposition. It is certainly true that, whilst the rain and the sun are essential for the growth of natural seed, the elements of the weather can also make for a hostile environment for a young plant to be growing in.

The world in which we live is a hostile spiritual environment and it is increasingly being noticed by believers across the world that opposition to the truth is increasing. It is vital, therefore, that we learn to persevere in the journey of faith, for it is only then that we will see the full release of God's blessing producing a good crop in and through our lives. Without using the third key of perseverance, so much of what we longed for in life could be lost.

Prayer: *Thank You, Lord, for the teaching that You have given us through the parables You told. Help me to not only hear the word and retain it in my heart, but also to persevere through all the difficulties and opposition I experience in life, so that at the end of my days there will be a good crop. In Jesus' name, Amen.*

Personal Notes

Day 23

God's Strategy for His Victories in My Life

'"As soon as you hear the sound of marching in the tops of the balsam trees, move quickly, because that will mean the LORD has gone out in front of you to strike the Philistine army." So David did as the LORD commanded him, and he struck down the Philistines all the way from Gibeon to Gezer.' 2 Samuel 5:24-25

The moment David was anointed King over Israel he became a target for the Philistines, the chief enemies of God's people in those days. The Philistines never forgot how David successfully killed Goliath with the first of his five smooth stones. There was no doubt that amongst the Philistines there were people with long memories for whom David was probably the most hated of men. He had removed from them their champion, Goliath, and now he had become King of Israel.

So the Philistines went up against King David *'in full force to search for him'*, (2 Samuel 5:17). But David was wise enough to ask the Lord what to do and as a result of David hearing the Lord's instruction, and then being obedient, the Philistines suffered a major defeat (2 Samuel 5:20-21). But before long the Philistines tried again. David might have thought "I'll just do what the Lord told us to do last time" – but if he had done that, he would have been defeated. David enquired of the Lord again what to do and God gave him a different strategy – to circle round the Philistine army and this time to attack them from behind.

Then the Lord gave David the specific instruction in today's scripture: Don't move until you hear a rustling (the sound of marching) in the tops of the trees – and when you do, then move quickly. Once again David was obedient to the Lord and had another major victory.

We can learn four vital lessons from this story. The first is this – whenever you face a difficulty, and don't know what to do, **ask the Lord**. Secondly, when you know that God has spoken, **obey**. Thirdly, don't presume that what happened last time will happen again – **return to the Lord** for fresh instruction, even if circumstances look the same. Then, fourthly, there will be times when you may need to **wait for a sign** from the Lord before you begin to act.

If we carefully apply these vital lessons from the Word of God in our daily battling against our spiritual enemy, then we can be confident that the Lord will go before us, as He did for David, and not only lead us into His victories, but also guide us into the place of His choosing.

I'd only just got my degree in chemistry and while I spent a year doing research I needed to earn some money. One Friday afternoon, I felt led to go to the local college of technology and offer my services to the chemistry department as a part-time teacher. The head of chemistry said he had no openings, but directed me along the corridor to the head of building, who needed someone urgently to start teaching a weekly class on building science that was beginning on Monday. The head of building turned out to be a Christian who was praying for an answer to his problem when I walked into his office!

I was the answer to his prayer and he was the answer to mine! It was the step that guided me into five years of college and university lecturing, prepared the way for fifteen years in business and then led to the establishment of Ellel Ministries. Huge consequences can result from apparently small decisions. I am so grateful that we have a God who loves us so much He wants to answer our prayers and guide our steps, just as He did for David.

Prayer: *Thank You, Lord, that You are a God who answers the prayers of Your children, when they look to You for guidance as David did. Help me, Lord, to be careful to listen to what You are saying to me, so that I will not fall into the traps of the enemy in the way I conduct my life. In Jesus' name, Amen.*

Personal Notes

Day 24

God's Blessing in Tough Times

'Blessed are those whose strength is in you [the Lord], who have set their hearts on pilgrimage. As they pass through the valley of Baca, they make it a place of springs, the autumn rains also cover it with pools. They go from strength to strength, till each appears before God in Zion.' Psalm 84:5-7

These three verses describe the journey of faith which believers follow as they travel through life. A pilgrimage is not an occasional walk in the country – it's a determined commitment to keep on walking forward in faith throughout life, until that moment comes when we step into the realms of glory and *'each appears before God in Zion'*. The psalmist states without any hint of compromise that those who set their hearts on pilgrimage will be blessed.

But almost immediately the psalmist anchors this promise of blessing into the context of earthly reality, as he recognises that none of us are exempt from the sufferings that are hinted at by reference to passing through *'the valley of Baca'*. The word 'Baca' means 'a place of tears', or 'a place of weeping and lamentation'. Tears are a godly expression of inner pain as we have to face pain for which there is no immediate answer. Tears are also the first step on the road to comfort and healing. A child who falls and is hurt will run in tears to mum or dad, where they are surrounded with arms of love, comfort and healing. We never cease to be God's children and His arms are always open in the valley of tears.

In this life, we are not exempt from the possibility of suffering, as is so graphically illustrated by Job's experiences, described in the first chapter of his book. There are many events in life that can be the source of pain and consequential tears.

One of the greatest sufferings we can experience is the untimely loss of a loved one. Such events prompt unanswerable questions – questions that Jesus totally understands. For, in the midst of the pain of bereavement, Jesus Himself declares, *'blessed are those who mourn, for they will be comforted.'* (Matthew 5:4). And how do we cope when we suffer disappointment, trauma, sickness, redundancy, or loss of any kind?

The valley of Baca is not only a place of tears. For our scripture then moves us on to the place of trusting God for the blessings that can come from Him. Such blessings can change *'the valley of Baca'* into *'a place of springs'* that strengthen and equip us for the onward journey of faith and encourage us to keep walking forward out of the valley.

My prayer today, therefore, is for all who are walking through your own personal *'valley of Baca'*, that in the midst of all the unanswerable questions you will keep looking up to the Lord in faith, knowing that He is the only source of comfort that can touch the very core of your being and strengthen our hearts for the pilgrimage that lies ahead. The springs that well up in the depths of the valley will enable us to go from strength to strength.

Prayer: *Thank You, Lord, that You understand the hurts and pains I experience when travelling through my personal 'valley of Baca'. Help me today to keep on trusting You on the pilgrimage of faith, even when things happen that I cannot understand. In Jesus' name, Amen.*

Personal Notes

Day 25

The Highway Code for God-Blessed Living!

'Where there is no revelation, the people cast off restraint; but blessed is he who keeps the law.' Proverbs 29:18

Restraints are for our good! Without having restraints in place there is danger. This is true in many areas of life. A road which passes along the edge of a precipice needs barriers by the side of the road to stop people driving over the edge. When there is heavy rain some areas of the country are subject to severe flooding and people's lives are at risk when flood waters become a raging torrent. A river is a wonderful blessing when it is contained within the restraint of its banks, but once that restraint has been breached the water goes everywhere, people's homes are flooded and there is danger. Restraints make the river safe. Restraints save lives.

In just the same way, the laws of God are meant to act as a restraint on our behaviour. But if people have no understanding that the restraints of God's law are designed to keep them safe, then they will have no reason to moderate their behaviour so as to live within those confines. Recently, our newspapers were full of news of the tragic death of one of Britain's richest women – she had everything she could possibly have wanted. Her house was said to have been worth seventy million pounds. But she and her husband had lived a life without restraint. They became addicted to drugs and, as a result, her life ended at a tragically early age. If only she had learned to live her life according to the revelation of truth that there is in the Word of God. Lack of restraint resulted in her premature death.

When we choose to respect that God's Word truly is a revelation from God Himself, and begin to walk in His ways, we lay down a foundation of blessing – not only for our own lives, but also for the lives of our children and grand-children. When we gladly live within those restraints we find ourselves constantly discovering the many blessings God wants us to enjoy as His children.

But because we have free-will, people find it tempting to laugh at those restraints and choose to live life in their own way. But they will eventually discover that the law of sowing and reaping applies to their lives. If you need convincing about the blessings that come to those who keep God's laws, then I suggest you spend a quiet hour reading Psalm 119. Just as the Highway Code is the blue-print for safe driving, Psalm 119 is the Highway Code for God-blessed living.

The Highway Code not only tells you what you must not do as a driver, but it also gives you good advice on how to drive safely. The Code provides both correction and direction. And in every area of life we need both. We need correction when things are going wrong and direction when we need to know how to live wisely. Pride says I don't want either – but humility gladly embraces both. God's correction and direction are life-giving and life-saving!

Prayer: *Thank You, Lord, that You loved us enough to show us how restraints can be a source of blessing in our lives. Help me, Lord, to welcome the application of Your laws in my life. In Jesus' name, Amen.*

Personal Notes

Day 26

Keep On Track

'My son, if sinners entice you, do not give in to them ... do not go along with them, do not set foot on their paths; for their feet rush into sin.' Proverbs 1:10, 15-16

The word 'entice' means 'to tempt', or 'to lead astray'. It carries with it all the connotations of exciting, but ungodly activities – things that fascinate the carnal nature and that, if we are honest, all of us can be vulnerable to from time to time. Everything from greed to lust, and a whole range of other strong desires, can get stirred up when enticement is in the air!

In these very testing days, when many people are struggling to hold things together financially, and many are having to fight depression, loneliness or a sense of despair, enticement is especially dangerous. People look for some form of 'comfort' or 'escape' from the pressures they are enduring and are much more vulnerable to temptations when they come – whether that temptation comes in the form of making money, having a wrong relationship, the false comfort of pornography or simply indulging in some other selfish but unproductive activity.

When times are tough, whether the season is totally personal to you or part of a national or international situation, the enemy will always try to take advantage of what's going on, to entice you into something ungodly. He does not want you to trust in God come what may, so He tries to stand in the place of God and be a source of comfort, not telling his victims that his sort of comfort will always prove to be false. Many is the person who has been led astray at times like this and ended up at a destination of their own choosing that was very different from God's best for their life.

Some have been financially ruined by falling for a supposed 'get-rich-quick' investment – and Christians are not exempt from being enticed by such schemes, which promise so much but realise so little. And many men, especially, have so indulged in viewing pornography that the images they have taken into their mind are a continuous source of taunting and fantasy temptation. Viewing pornography breaks a sacred trust between husband and wife and provides a very ungodly spiritual inheritance for children.

While today's pornography was not available when Jesus taught His followers He was, nevertheless, very well aware of the problem, otherwise He wouldn't have needed to say that *"anyone who looks on a woman lustfully has already committed adultery with her in his heart"* (Matthew 5:27).

When John penned the letters from Jesus to the seven Churches (see Revelation 2 and 3) each one highlighted issues and problems that needed dealing with in the churches. However, they also each ended with strong words of encouragement to endure and overcome. Jesus knew that, in testing times, the enemy would want to rob them of their inheritance. So, I urge you not to let anyone be used by the enemy to entice you away and rob you of your inheritance in God. Press on, win through and keep running the race of life!

Prayer: *Help me, Lord, to recognise the enticements of the enemy when they come and then to endure and overcome whatever obstacles stand in the way of my destiny in God. In Jesus' name, Amen.*

Personal Notes

A Matter of Choice

'"Now fear the LORD and serve him with faithfulness. Throw away the gods your forefathers worshiped beyond the River and in Egypt and serve the LORD. But if serving the LORD seems undesirable to you, then choose for yourselves this day whom you will serve, whether the gods your forefathers served beyond the River, or the gods of the Amorites in whose land you are living. But as for me and my household, we will serve the LORD."'
Joshua 24:14-15

Joshua gave the people of God three choices – you can either vote for the gods of Egypt, the gods of the Amorites or the Lord! No, it wasn't an election, but the people were being challenged by their leader to make a choice and there were three obvious choices they could make. "Who are you going to serve?" Joshua asked. He also made it very clear that as their leader there was no doubting the choice he was making – he, and all his household, were going to serve the Lord.

When a nation elects a political party to govern their country, they have to live with the consequences of their choice. And similarly, when we choose which 'god or gods' we are going to serve, we have to live with the consequences of that choice also. The election of a political party only gives them power for a relatively short period of time. But when we choose the gods that we are going to serve, the consequences can go beyond the realms of time and affect our eternal destiny as well.

The gods of Egypt and the gods of the Amorites had already been proven to be false gods, but the problem with false gods is that they can be very attractive; they can be made to fit in with whatever lifestyle or morality you would like to have! It's easy to follow a god who lets you do whatever you like, without reference to whether that is either good for you or right. False gods always distort the truth and sell you a lie.

When Moses was away for so long up the mountain receiving instruction from God, the people decided they would make a god of their own. So, they all contributed items of gold and made a golden calf. They celebrated with eating, drinking and revelry and God had to tell Moses that the people had become corrupt (see Exodus 32). Anything that assumes a greater significance in our lives than God Himself has already begun to turn our hearts away from following Him.

The Lord is not a false god, He is the living God whose love and laws provide the boundaries of safety for the whole of mankind. If we choose to follow and serve Him, we may sometimes find that His Word says 'No' to things our flesh would want to say 'Yes' to. But serving false gods can be a bit like voting for a god who encourages us to say 'Yes' to the things that will destroy us from the inside out and eventually rob us of life itself.

It's not only time to seek the Lord, it's time for those who know and love Him to vote with their feet and turn away from the gods of this world and keeping their focus on the Lord - and Him alone! His is the very best government for our lives, under which we will be secure for time and eternity.

Prayer: *Thank You, Lord God, that You are totally trustworthy and that Your love and Your laws provide all those who choose to follow You with security for time and eternity. I choose, this day, to love and serve the Lord! In Jesus' name, Amen.*

Personal Notes

Day 28

Partial Obedience is Disobedience!

'So God said to Noah ... make yourself an ark ... this is how you are to build it. The ark is to be 450 feet long, 75 feet wide and 45 feet high ...' Genesis 6:13-15

God not only asked Noah to build a boat, He also gave him very detailed instructions about the size of the vessel and how the ark was to be built. It was to be a for a very specific purpose and had to be large enough to take on board the biggest floating menagerie the world has ever seen – either before or since!

When Noah heard God speaking to him, he could easily have said, "Yes, Lord, I'll build a boat – but I think you must have got the design a bit wrong, I think it would be best if I made a few alterations to the plans!" He might have set to work to build a vessel and done it, in Frank

Sinatra style, *'My Way!'* And when the boat was finished it would have turned out to be a magnificent pleasure yacht for him and his family! Noah could have said that he had been totally obedient to God by building a boat, but in reality he would have been disobedient: he'd have built a boat to his own design, for his own pleasure instead of to fulfil God's purposes.

When the flood came and God told him to gather on board two of every animal under the sun, Noah's pleasure craft would have proved woefully inadequate for the task. His partial obedience would have destroyed God's plan. It would have been no good Noah protesting to God that at least he built a boat since what he had built was totally useless for its purposee it – it would have been totally useless as a result of his sinful disobedience.

When you read the stories of the kings of Judah and Israel you find many short comments about their lives. One of which says that *'Amaziah did what was right in the eyes of the* Lord, *but not wholeheartedly'* (2 Chronicles 25:2). Eventually Amaziah turned away from the Lord and finally he lost his life in tragic circumstances! For him partial obedience brought his life to a sudden end.

And for most of Jehoshaphat's life He was a good king. He had even experienced the fear of the Lord coming on his enemies and, as a result, there was peace on every side of his kingdom (2 Chronicles 20:29-30). But then Jehoshaphat made an alliance for a business deal with an evil king, contrary to the will of God for him. The result was an unmitigated disaster (2 Chronicles 20:35-37).

It's vital that, when we are clear God has spoken to us and shown us from His Word the way to live and what He wants us to be and to do, we don't compromise with partial obedience. Each of our lives is a vessel that, like Noah, we are building day by day. We have a destiny to fulfil, but partial obedience will always mean that we're never quite fit for the Master's use and it could have serious, even disastrous, consequences.

Prayer: *Thank You, Lord, for these powerful lessons from Scripture. I'm sorry, Lord, for times in my life when I have been less than wholehearted in following You and have, as a result, only been partially obedient. Forgive me, Lord, for this disobedience and help me to start again, with Your help, and build the right vessel for the purposes You have for me in the future. In Jesus' name, Amen.*

Personal Notes

Day 29

Is it Time to Get Moving?

'The Lord your God said to us at Horeb, "You have stayed long enough at this mountain. Break camp and advance into the hill country of the Amorites" ... See, I have given you this land. Go in and take possession.' Deuteronomy 1:6, 8

I was once given some wise advice – stay where you are until the Lord moves you on. But when He pushes, get moving! The fact is, if we stay put when the Lord has said 'move', we will always miss out on God's best for us.

The time had come for Moses to move on in his extraordinary pilgrimage through the desert with approximately two million Israelites – God had a purpose, great blessing and a destination for them. Sadly, they all missed the blessing by refusing to do what God had said. As a result they spent forty years wandering through the desert wilderness before they reached their destination.

I will never forget talking with an elderly man who told me all the times that God had spoken to him about leaving his business job and responding to the call on his life to be a missionary. It was a very sad tale. For as he told me the story I was thinking about all the things he could have done for the Lord, had he been obedient – and all the eternal rewards he had missed out on by staying put when God had told him to move. His 'desert pilgrimage' had also been forty years, and a bit more.

I often think about that man and I pray now that, as you read this, you will take the opportunity to make sure you are in the place of God's calling and appointing. If so, that's good. Otherwise, this may be a time when God is saying to you 'You have stayed long enough at this mountain …' It's great to stay put if God has said this is your place. It's just as great to move on when he says 'move'. If God is encouraging you to move, pray for the His wisdom about when and where to move to, so that you will be sure to end up at the right destination – in God's timing and not yours.

The great pioneering missionary, C T Studd had done extraordinary work in China with Hudson Taylor's China Inland Mission. This was followed by years of pioneering service in India, at the end of which he was in very poor health and was invalided home, presumably to live out the rest of his days in the peace and quiet of England.

But God had other ideas. Studd was restless to take the next step of obedience, believing there was yet more for him to do. Even though his mission board totally opposed the suggestion, he began to plan for a further faith journey to take the gospel into central Africa. Notwithstanding his poor health, he established a major mission bridgehead in central Africa in the early part of the twentieth century, established the great missionary society Worldwide Evangelisation Crusade and twenty years later he was laid to rest in Africa having opened the doors for untold millions to eventually find Christ.

C T Studd knew when it was time for the Lord to move him on. He obeyed and, in spite of massive difficulties along the way, countless blessings followed. When God says go, it's time to move!

Prayer: *Thank You, Lord, that You love me enough to give me a push when I need to move on. Help me to be always listening for Your gentle voice so that I can know from You what it is You want me to do and when to start moving towards Your objective for my life. In Jesus' name, Amen.*

Personal Notes

Day 30

Living Water and Crack-Free Cisterns!

'My people have committed two sins: They have forsaken me, the spring of living water, and have dug their own cisterns, broken cisterns that cannot hold water.' Jeremiah 2:13

There were many different things that God's people did when they turned their back on the living God. They began to lose their covering and protection – essential requirements for knowing the ongoing guidance of the living God. The list of sins that would describe all their ungodly activities would have been very long! But when, through the prophet Jeremiah, God began to speak words of rebuke, he reduced all their sinful behaviour into just two categories.

Firstly, they had deserted the only source of living water and **secondly**, they had tried to generate their own 'water supply' as a substitute for the living water that flows from the heart of God.

In Israel, underground cisterns were vital for the storage of water ready for the dry season. Without a good cistern people would die of dehydration. A cracked cistern was useless. Water would flow into it but the water would leak away through the cracks so that, when the water was most needed, there would be none there.

God uses this picture to speak to His people about what they had been doing. He uses the need for physical water as a parable of the need for the living spiritual water, which sustains God's people through all the ups and downs of life. The first sin of God's people was to decide that they wanted an alternative source of supply. So, instead of constantly coming back to the only source of living water, they did what mankind has tried to do throughout history – they built their own cistern, which included everything from idolatry to sexual immorality.

They finished up believing that good was bad and bad was good, and going in the opposite direction to the ways of God. This is what Isaiah said: *'Woe to those who call evil good and good evil, who put darkness for light and light for darkness, who put bitter for sweet and sweet for bitter'* (Isaiah 5:20).

God had provided for them everything they needed to live in a covenant relationship with Him, who had created the world and everything in it. But pride in the heart of man will always want to build an alternative way, and say it's better than what God provided in the first place.

Ultimately, this is the foundation for every alternative belief system, false religion or moral order that has ever risen up in the heart of man and been practised on the face of the earth.

It's easy to look at the people of Israel and ask, "How could they?" But all we need to do is look at our own generation and see that twenty-first century man is no different. The reason that I wrote the series of books *Journey to Freedom*, and why I believe God put the vision for it into my heart, was to help those in need of healing to seek a constant flow of living water from God's Word. Then they won't be wanting to build an alternative, but cracked, cistern in their lives which has no capacity to be the spiritual resource which is so vital for each and every one of us.

Prayer: Help me, Lord, to only ever want the living water which flows from Your heart to the heart of man. And give me the determination to rebuild sound and crack-free cisterns in my own life, so that the Water of Life will always be available to me throughout my days – even in seasons of drought. In Jesus' name, Amen.

Personal Notes

Day 31

When Waiting is Safer than Acting

'I am still confident of this: I will see the goodness of the LORD in the land of the living. Wait for the LORD; be strong and take heart and wait for the LORD.' Psalm 27:13-14

David had many enemies and he faced many battles. At times he was on the run and situations seemed hopeless. But throughout all his trials and difficulties he never forgot the lessons of his early years, lessons he had learnt while looking after his father's sheep. The Lord was close to him and he had learned to trust that inner voice of God, which had been his steadfast defence on so many occasions. God had shown him what to do when defending his flock from the lion and the bear. David had learnt by experience that he could really trust the voice of his God.

David's words, from today's scripture, were not just

religious words without serious meaning; they were his own lifetime experience. He was passing on his experience of God to others and training them in the fact that even if things look pretty black, God can be trusted and it is better to wait for God than to take things into our own hands, act hastily and turn away from trusting in Him.

Many years ago I was in the middle of a business crisis. I was under personal physical threat and my business was on the edge of bankruptcy. It would have been easy to turn my back on God and blame Him for my problems, when in reality the mess was a result of my own mistake. But God heard my cry and on the very day that my accuser began to threaten my life, God delivered me from him in the most miraculous of ways. I felt like a bird that had been released from a trap; I was free, I could fly again. God had given me another chance.

I have never forgotten that experience. It is etched on my memory for ever. I learnt in the extremes of near disaster that to be strong and wait for the Lord is not just good advice – on some occasions, it is life-saving advice!

As I am writing this, I am conscious that some people reading this may well be locked in a difficult situation of their own, with no obvious way out. May I encourage you to face every aspect of the situation head on. If there are mistakes you've made you need to confess those to the Lord and ask for forgiveness and put anything right that hasn't yet been corrected. If there are people you need to forgive because of what they've done, then don't delay. And if there's nothing more you can do, then commit your ways and every aspect of the situation into the Lord's hands, put your trust in Him and wait for Him to act.

The Lord delivered David on many occasions out of the hand of his enemies. His experiences were not mere entertaining stories – they were, literally, about situations when David could have died. God was faithful, He acted and David was delivered.

Prayer: *Thank You, Lord, that You are a God who hears and answers prayer. Help me to be patient as I wait for You. I choose to trust You in a new way today and look forward to your answer to the cries of my heart. In Jesus' name, Amen.*

Personal Notes

Day 32

Honest and Dishonest Dealing

'You must have accurate and honest weights and measures, so that you may live long in the land the LORD your God is giving you. For the LORD your God detests anyone who does these things, anyone who deals dishonestly.' Deuteronomy 25:15-16

The Bible contains some very surprising things. An example is our scripture today! In these instructions to His people, God makes a direct correlation between honesty (or lack of it) and how long people might live. Superficially, what possible connection can there be between selling someone short and the length of time your body is able to live?

Such things make no sense at all if you only think of the body as existing in isolation and independent from the person whose body it is. But from Genesis to Revelation there is a message that runs through the whole of the Bible

– sin has its consequences, and those consequences can be worked out through the flesh. Our spirit, soul and body are all different dimensions of the same created order. What happens to one, affects the others.

When a trader gives short measure through using false weights, it is a form of stealing. The trader is making a conscious choice to ignore the voice of God within (their conscience). Thus their whole being becomes involved in the deception. There is another divine law which says that how we treat others is the way we ourselves will be treated. So, if a trader sells his customer short, it makes total sense that his life might be shortened as a result! What happens in reality is that when we choose to act deceitfully like this, we are turning our back on the protection of God.

In the story of Daniel, we read how he was put into the lion's den as a result of his obedience to God and not to the king. But then we read that Daniel was unharmed because God sent His angel to shut the mouths of the lions and that it was Daniel's innocence before God that gave him this special protection (Daniel 6:21).

Deceiving others for our own selfish gain gives the enemy greater access to our lives and he is a thief and a robber. It's better always to deal honestly in all our relationships and never to cheat anyone out of what is their right. Satan will use the rights we give him to steal from us.

Zacchaeus got the message loud and clear. He was challenged by the straight and uncompromising teaching of Jesus and became convicted about all the taxes he had collected which were more than he should have done. Immediately, he undertook to repay people four-fold (Luke 19:8). God was powerfully at work in his life. No wonder Jesus was happy to go and stay in his house! (Matthew 19:5).

Jesus considered stealing from others, in any way whatsoever, a very serious issue. So, should we.

Prayer: *Help me, Lord, to remember any times when I have not been fair and honest in any of my dealings. And then give me the courage to put things right before You and with whoever it is that I've wronged. In Jesus' name, Amen.*

Personal Notes

Day 33

God's Confirming Word

'Write down the revelation and make it plain on tablets, so that a herald may run with it. For the revelation awaits an appointed time …' Habakkuk 2:2-3

I have often been amazed at the way God uses scripture to confirm the guidance and visions that He puts into my heart. God gave me a very clear vision that God wanted Ellel Ministries to publish an online training school, so that the foundational teaching, which has been so instrumental in blessing people wherever the work has been established, could be available online to people anywhere in the world at the click of their computer mouse!

When God speaks like that you begin to look for confirmation that this really is from God, for you don't want to be spending a lot of time and energy in developing something that was only a good idea, and not God's idea. Shortly after this I was visiting America and one of the team handed me a piece of paper with the above scripture written on it. She said the Lord had given it to her for me personally.

I was totally amazed when I looked it up. *'Make the revelation plain ... write it down on tablets.'* The revelation of an online training school certainly had to be written down, otherwise there would be nothing to communicate. In Habakkuk's day a tablet meant a wax covered piece of wood on which a message could be scratched. Today's tablets are computer files. *'So that a herald may run with it'.* The herald is no longer a man with legs, but the internet which can send the messages on computer files to every country of the world in seconds.

I was stunned as I read this message from the Lord to me, delivered by a person who had no idea what I was thinking about at the time. This was God's very clear confirmation to me that the vision really was from the Lord. God is amazing. He really does use His Word to speak to us in the twenty-first century! At a later date the online teaching, originally published as *Ellel 365*, was made available in print as *Journey to Freedom*.

Before the work even started and I was looking in Scripture for teaching on healing that I would give people who came on our healing retreats, the Lord highlighted to me Luke 9:11. Here, Luke tells us that Jesus welcomed the people, taught them about the Kingdom of God and healed those in need.

Those three simple principles – welcome, teach the Kingdom of God and pray for healing became the foundational heart of the ministry. God showed me that unless people are welcomed and loved they won't listen to the teaching they need to hear. And that it is the teaching about the Kingdom of God (the truth) that they then need to apply in their lives, which opens their hearts to God's healing. Then they discover that, as Jesus said, *'the truth will set you free'* (John 8:31).

God uses His Word as a means of guidance throughout our lives. But, if we don't read it He can't use it. If we get it into our hearts through reading it, the Holy Spirit can then 'get it out' to direct our steps.

Prayer: *Thank You, Lord, that You continue to speak to Your people through Your Word. Help me to read it with the understanding that comes from Your Spirit, so that I can hear Your voice speaking into my heart to confirm those things that are of You. In Jesus' name, Amen.*

Personal Notes

Day 34

Whose Plans are You Following?

'Do not put your trust in princes, in mortal men who cannot save. When their spirit departs, they return to the ground and on that very day their plans come to nothing.' Psalm 146:3-4

It's a sad but true fact that most unfulfilled plans that have their origin in man come to an end when the person dies. So the psalmist encourages us not to put our trust in men, whoever they may be, for they cannot save us and, in the end, all their plans will come to nothing.

So, if even princes can't be trusted to help us, who can we trust? When you look at the plans of God that unfolded throughout the Old Testament and then into the New, we see that God's plans were continued from one generation to the next. Prophecies spoken about Jesus were fulfilled. Those visions that had their origin in God and not man did not die but were taken up in a sort of spiritual relay race down the centuries. One person after another took up the baton of faith and continued to fulfil the purposes of God. Take a look at the astounding record of the saints of God described in Hebrews chapter 11.

There is an important lesson for us here at a personal level. If we are following our own plans for our lives, then their potential will be limited. But if we are following God's plans and walking forward in the vision that comes from Him, then we can be absolutely sure that nothing of what we do for the Kingdom in this way will ever be wasted. What we achieve for Him will build on what others have done and in time others will build on what we do.

I love telling the story of the effects of D L Moody's conversion to Christ in the basement of a Boston shoe store on 21 April 1855. He became a prominent evangelist and visited England on several occasions. In 1875 he preached in a London theatre and Edward Studd, a wealthy business man and race-horse owner, was converted. A year later, Studd's three sons were also converted, one of whom C T Studd, became a renowned missionary evangelist and another, Kynaston, became the Lord Mayor of London.

Kynaston Studd, now Sir Kynaston and the Lord Mayor of London, conducted Christian House Parties for young men in Switzerland. My Dad went to one in 1937, staying in a hotel by the shores of Lake Lucerne. My Mum was also staying there from South Africa, on her way to London for the coronation of King George VI. My Mum and Dad met, married the following year and the rest is history. Were it not for the man who led D L Moody to Christ in the basement of the shoe store, none of what God has done through Ellel Ministries could have happened.

So, be encouraged, listen carefully to the heart of God and measure His heartbeat against your own – are they in tune with each other? If they are, never fear, you are building for the generations of time as well as for eternity and one day the treasure you have laid down will be waiting for you!

Prayer: Help me, Lord, to walk in Your ways and to listen to Your voice. I want my life to be lived in line with the plans that have their origin in You and not to waste my life doing things with no future! In Jesus' name, Amen.

Personal Notes

Day 35

Chosen to Wait!

'Sovereign Lord, as you have promised, dismiss now your servant in peace. For my eyes have seen your salvation, which you prepared in the sight of all people, a light for revelation to the Gentiles and for glory to your people Israel.' Luke 2:29-32

Simeon and Anna were elderly. They had gone to the temple daily all their lives and other than the daily worship of God, there was only one item on Simeon's agenda. He was looking at all the babies that were being brought to the temple to be presented to the Lord. I can easily imagine him looking intently at every one, asking the same old question of the Lord, day in and day out, "Is this THE one?"

There had always been an assurance in Simeon's heart that he wouldn't die before he saw this special baby being presented. But until that day the answer had always been "No". Today was different. There was a quickening in his spirit, an assurance in his heart and then he found himself speaking out words that only God could have given him. His eyes had seen the very salvation of God as he held this babe from heaven in his arms.

And so he told the world, and all subsequent generations, that the promise of the prophets had been fulfilled. Salvation had come, the Light for the Gentiles, the glory for Israel – people could now look forward to redemption. Then Anna, a prophetess, added her affirmation to what Simeon had said and *'spoke about the child to all who were looking forward to the redemption of Jerusalem'* (Luke 2:38).

Simeon and Anna were only asked to do one thing by the Lord – provide prophetic witness to the identity of the child in Joseph and Mary's arms. But every generation of believers since has remembered what they said and did!

What an encouragement that must be to us – to watch and wait patiently for the fulfilment of the destiny God has for each one of us. He may have many things for us to do or, like Simeon and Anna, there may only be one major responsibility planned, but our faithfulness will bring great blessing, even to many generations.

Back in 1970 God gave me the vision for the work that became Ellel Ministries. For sixteen years I prayed daily into the vision. Many times, I thought of ways that I could give God a nudge and help Him with His plans. But each time I did that my ideas fell through. It was only when, in 1986, I was led to a building called Ellel Grange that it became transparently clear that the time had come and this was the place. God's ideas were best. And during those sixteen years of waiting there were many things that God had to take me through by way of preparation. If I had acted hastily it would have been premature and I wouldn't have been ready. There is both a time for waiting and a time for acting.

When the right day – and the right baby – came, Simeon lifted up his eyes to heaven and spoke out those amazing words of declaration – light had come into the world!

Prayer: *Thank You for the faithfulness of Simeon and Anna. Help me Lord to remain faithful to You in all things as I await the fulfilment of my own destiny in God. In Jesus' name, Amen.*

Personal Notes

Day 36

Are you a Finisher?

'Tell Archippus: "See to it that you complete the work you have received in the Lord."' Colossians 4:17

There are many interesting spiritual lessons in the little greetings which Paul includes at the end of his letters. In this scripture he is adding a personal message for an individual, who is described in Paul's letter to Philemon as a fellow-soldier.

We have no idea why Paul felt this personal message was necessary, but the most likely reason is that Archippus was a person who was good at starting things, but not so good at carrying them through to completion. If that's the case, then he is typical of many people, even in the body of Christ, who get really excited about something new, but show little enthusiasm for persevering with what's already on the go!

It's exciting when God calls us into something, but it's not so exciting when we discover that there is opposition to face, hardships and sacrifice along the way and much work to be done to realise the potential God has opened up for us. The fruit of our calling does not appear out of the sky, delivered by an angel, like a bit of Hollywood magic! It has to be worked for through loving obedience to the One who called us into His service.

When Paul was describing the difficulties he had experienced in 2 Corinthians 11, he listed everything from shipwreck to beatings at the hands of both Romans and Jews and an attempt on his life by stoning. Shipwrecks, hunger, nakedness, lack of sleep were just some of the many things he suffered as he pressed on *'toward the goal to win the prize for which God has called me heavenward in Christ Jesus'* (Philippians 3:14).

And in the case of Jesus, it was the final act of His life, His sacrifice on the cross, that made sense of the rest of His life! Hebrews describes Jesus as *'the author and finisher of our faith'* (Hebrews 12:2). Because Jesus finished the task that Father God had given Him, His destiny was fulfilled. Jesus was the most amazing example of a completer-finisher. Hebrews urges us to look to Jesus, follow His example and walk in His steps.

Many years ago, we obediently took the work of Ellel Ministries into Hungary for two very successful conferences, which attracted people from all over the former Soviet Union. But that wasn't God's ultimate objective for us. If we hadn't persevered and then found a piece of land on which to build a centre, the work that has now spread right across Central and Eastern Europe as far as Siberia would have been stopped in its tracks. We had to complete the first stage of the guidance God had given, before we could see where He wanted us to go next.

So, if there is something that you know God has given you to do, keep going. Persevere and complete the task. It is that final stage of the journey that will result in the greatest blessing and fruit.

If Paul was writing a letter to you – what would he say? Would he have a message for you like he had for Archippus?

Prayer: *Lord, help me to persevere with the things that You ask me to do. I don't want my life to be marked by many new starts but with nothing ever finished. Teach me how to keep on putting my foot down in Your footprints, day by day, till I fulfil Your purposes for my life. In Jesus' name, Amen.*

Personal Notes

Day 37

All the Days of My Life!

'You prepare a table before me in the presence of my enemies. You anoint my head with oil; my cup overflows. Surely goodness and love will follow me all the days of my life, and I will dwell in the house of the LORD forever.' Psalm 23:5-6

All of us have a measure of time stretching out ahead of us, but none of us knows exactly how long it will be. It could be days, weeks, months or many years. But however many or few those days are, the encouragement to live every day as if it is our last, is sound spiritual advice.

For if we knew that today, for example, was the very day on which we would be meeting the Lord face to face, we would not, under any circumstances, want to be involved in ungodly things when His call came! And that being the case, it is worth asking the question why would we ever want to be involved in doing ungodly things? Not just because our home call may come any time soon, but because, surely, we love the Lord and would always want to walk in His ways? Walking in His ways is a foundational principle of the guidance of God.

I have, sadly, come to the conclusion that one of the main reasons many Christians get thrown off course by continuing to fall into sin, is because they love themselves more than they love the Lord. When self-indulgence takes priority over relational obedience it's very easy to get diverted from God's best by the temptations that come our way because of our carnal nature.

The spiritual reality of daily life is that we are, at all times, living in a world that has sold its soul to the god of this world and that we are, therefore, always in the midst of spiritual enemies. Those enemies are, ultimately, God's enemies. But because we are in Him and He is in us, they are our enemies also.

So, while self-indulgent temptations are a constant threat and potential discouragement, our scripture for today should be a constant encouragement to us. It simply tells us that even in the midst of our enemies God is there for us. Or, in the words of the psalmist, He prepares a table for us exactly where we are! So we don't need to give in to self-indulgence to provide us with false comfort – for God has promised to be our Provider, even in the midst of our enemies.

We have faced many different attacks and difficulties over our years in ministry, but times God has always encouraged us not to run away because of the enemy, but to keep pressing on with His calling and purposes. In the practical reality of daily Christian ministry we have seen how God has laid out a spread of provision for our needs right where we are! He has continued to anoint us for the work of bringing healing to those in need and our cup of thanksgiving has overflowed.

All that God has done in the past is a huge encouragement to press on in the present with whatever it is that He has called us to do. He will always be there for us throughout our days. And, even better, at the end of our days we are assured that we will dwell with Him in the house of the Lord forever.

So, even if the days ahead may look difficult, there is constant reason to give thanks to the Lord and to follow Paul's advice to *'rejoice in the Lord always ... do not be anxious about anything, but in everything by prayer and petition, with thanksgiving, present your requests to God. And the peace of God, which transcends all understanding, will guard your hearts and your minds in Christ Jesus'* (Philippians 4:4-7).

Prayer: *Thank You, Lord, for the assurance of Your presence with me for all of my days and the promise of Your provision and encouragement every step of the way, until I can share in the joy, with You, of my eternal home with the saints of God. In Jesus' name, Amen.*

Personal Notes

Day 38

Unfailing Love – our Guide for Ever

'Within your temple, O God, we meditate on your unfailing love ... For this God is our God for ever and ever; he will be our guide even to the end.' Psalm 48:9, 14

The love of God is timeless – it never fails. God IS love and His love never runs out. And His promise to guide us throughout all our days is without limitation. We never cease to be loved. We can know that whatever happens in life, His promises remain true to the end of our days.

We need not fear that God will cease to value us or lose interest when we are no longer in either the flush of youth or at the peak of our potential in the middle of life. He loves us when we are young and He loves us when we are old.

I was once privileged to pray with an elderly saint of God. A man who had faithfully served God throughout a lifetime in ministry and for close on another twenty years of service beyond official retirement. He knew that he was dying and after talking to him for a little while, I asked him what he would like me to pray for at this critical stage of his life. I might have expected him to suggest a range of family needs, or personal issues associated with his condition. But I was completely taken aback when he said, "there's only one thing, pray that I will finish well!"

Even when Jesus was on the cross, at the end of His earthly life, Satan was tempting Him to use His power and authority to come down off the cross. If He had done so, Jesus would have come under Satan's authority and His sacrificial death would have been to no avail. It was vital that Jesus died without sin, so that death could have no hold over Him. Even in His dying moments, therefore, Jesus needed to be on His guard against taking a wrong step.

The temptation to go off course is always there – even when we are old. And my friend who was dying, was still wanting to be sure that he was putting his feet down each day in the place God had planned and purposed for him, even at the very end of his days. He died well.

The Christian life is not like a career in which we may work during the days of our employment and then retire from at the age of sixty-five! There is no retirement from the Christian life and our latter years, when we don't have the commitments of regular employment, can be the most fruitful of our whole lives, when we have the opportunity to use all our days – right up to the end – to sow seeds into the lives of others. Those seeds can bear fruit on earth long after we have entered glory.

You may be approaching that season of your life when you are thinking about retirement or are already retired. I pray that you will take a fresh look at all the years that still lie ahead and seek God's guidance anew as to how you may pray and plan for those years to be fruitful for the Kingdom of God. Personal indulgence, without consideration of what God might have in store for those years, may rob Him of the opportunity to pour out His blessings on others and you of the chance to enhance your personal treasure chest in Heaven!

God has promised to be our Guide until the end – let's not ignore His directions as we continue to put our feet down for Him. As long as we have breath we have a purpose to live for!

Prayer: *Thank You, Jesus, for the amazing promises we find in the Bible – promises that God will be our guide, even until the very end of our lives. Help me, Lord, to have eyes and ears open to see what You are doing and to hear Your voice, so that I will not miss out on any of the blessings and opportunities that You have stored up for me in each and every stage of my life. In Jesus' name, Amen.*

Personal Notes

_____

_____

_____

_____

_____

_____

_____

_____

_____

_____

_____

_____

_____

_____

_____

_____

_____

_____

_____

_____

_____

_____

_____

_____

_____

Day 39

God's Perspective

'The Sovereign LORD *is my strength; he makes my feet like the feet of a deer, he enables me to go on the heights.'* Habakkuk 3:19

In order to see the view, you need to get up high! Situations that look difficult from below can suddenly seem very different from an elevated perspective.

I recently went on a long walk with my son and his family. The four grandchildren were full of energy as their Dad led us to the top of a steep hill – easier for them than for me! But when we got to the top, the view was worth every one of our many uphill steps. As I looked down on the valley below and out to the sea beyond, I realised afresh that God's view is always from the high places. There is nothing hidden from His sight and as long as we remain in Him, then we will be able to see things from His perspective.

A deer has no difficulty in climbing the heights and jumping over obstacles. It is a perfect picture of how we need to be in God. Energised by Him, He enables us to do more than we would have thought possible. Gaining the heights is sometimes costly and time consuming, but the heights God has prepared for us are always achievable when He envisions and empowers us.

God is our strength. He makes our feet to be like those of a deer. He enables us to go on to the heights, to see things from His perspective and overcome the obstacles the enemy puts in our way. There is nothing more encouraging than to have His viewpoint on all the issues and stages of life's journey.

How do we get God's viewpoint? A vital key is to read God's Word day by day – letting the truth about God soak into our spirit and learning how it is that His ways are more trustworthy than ours. Isaiah summed up God's perspective in these words: '"For my thoughts are not your thoughts, neither are your ways my ways," declares the Lᴏʀᴅ. "As the heavens are higher than the earth, so are my ways higher than your ways and my thoughts than your thoughts"' (Isaiah 55:8-9).

In 2 Chronicles 25:2, Amaziah is described as a king who *'did what was right in the eyes of the Lᴏʀᴅ, but not wholeheartedly.'* He wanted to serve the Lord, but at times he would choose to do things his way when it suited him. This was a recipe for disaster that eventually cost Amaziah his life!

Wherever you find people in scripture telling God that His

ways are not the best ways, you will soon find that the end result is not good. Arrogance and pride are never a good substitute for humility and obedience. Verse 20 of this chapter says it very plainly, *'Amaziah, however, would not listen.'*

The real issue for Amaziah was an unwillingness to come under authority. As king, he was in charge of the country and God was his ultimate authority. But in his pride he turned away from the Lord. He failed to remain in God and see things from His perspective. The rebellion at the root of his lack of wholeheartedness eventually destroyed him. It was as if dark clouds came across his spiritual eyes and he lost his ability to see things from God's perspective.

Staying close to God, being whole-hearted for Him and seeing things from His point of view will not only enable us to see beyond our immediate circumstances, but will ensure that the guidance of God remains our source of daily direction throughout our lives.

Prayer: *Thank You, Lord, that You invite me to be in You and to see things from Your perspective. Help me to stay close to You all day and every day. I don't want sinful wilfulness to draw clouds across my sight, so that I cannot see the right way to go. I choose to walk with You on the high places. In Jesus' name, Amen.*

Personal Notes

_____

_____

_____

_____

_____

_____

_____

_____

_____

_____

_____

_____

_____

_____

_____

_____

_____

_____

_____

_____

_____

_____

_____

Day 40

God Has a Plan!

'The day for building your walls will come, the day for extending your boundaries.' Micah 7:11

When the prophet Micah wrote these words, the land and the people were in devastation. God had not spared His own beloved people from the consequences of their own sins. There was always a day of reckoning for rebellion. Even today, when we live in days of New Covenant grace, we are still not exempt from the consequences of our own choices when they take us away from God.

But, even though His people had sinned grievously, God did not stop loving them. And, in time, it was the consequences of their mistakes which eventually brought them to their senses, and they turned back to God in repentance. This was the essence of the story Jesus told about the prodigal son. When the son came back home the father threw a party of celebration and thanksgiving. Repentance is always the beginning of hope and the doorway to God's ongoing plan for His people.

Whatever there may have been in our past, God has not stopped loving His people today. He has not changed His character. He still loves us in spite of the mistakes we may have made. And, as in Micah's day, God looks forward in anticipation to a time of rebuilding.

So, if you are looking at your own life, even if it's a scene of your own personal devastation, or praying for someone who's going through a tough time, remember, God is a Redeemer. He can see beyond the mess, He has a plan – and if we put our hand afresh into His, then we will soon be able to see what God can already see and discover the plans of God for our lives.

When I started restoring the crashed car, through which God gave me the vision for the work of Ellel Ministries, I needed an original plan, a blue-print, of the maker's design. Without this I couldn't know exactly what the maker had intended for the car. But with this in my hand I could begin the work. God has the equivalent of a blue-print for our lives – He has a plan and I believe it brings great joy to His heart to see His children coming to Him for personal restoration according to His plans.

And just in case you may be thinking that He has a plan for everyone else, but not for you, let me encourage you by saying that there are no exceptions – God has a plan for your life as well. On Day One of our journey, we were reminded in Jeremiah 29:11 that He has plans to give us a hope and a future.

Just as David encouraged the people, telling them to *'lift up your heads, O you gates, be lifted up you ancient doors, that the King of Glory may come in'* (Psalm 24:7), I would encourage you also to lift up your head towards the Lord so that He, the King of Glory, may come in and enter every corner of your life.

God is the 'Restorer-in Chief' and He will bring about His plans for your life as you watch Him at work, guiding you into the next stage of your own personal journey. The day for building the walls of your life will come as you extend your boundaries and venture into all that the Lord has prepared for you.

Prayer: *Thank You, Lord, that You have a plan for each one of our lives, including mine. Help me to see beyond all my circumstances and to trust You so that there will be a new day of building walls and extending boundaries in my life. In Jesus' name, Amen.*

Personal Notes

_____

_____

_____

_____

_____

_____

Ellel Ministries
International

About Ellel Ministries

Our Vision
Ellel Ministries is a non-denominational Christian Mission Organization with a vision to resource and equip the Church by welcoming people, teaching them about the Kingdom of God and healing those in need (Luke 9:11).

Our Mission
Our mission is to fulfil the above vision throughout the world, as God opens the doors, in accordance with the Great Commission of Jesus and the calling of the Church to proclaim the Kingdom of God by preaching the good news, healing the broken-hearted and setting the captives free. We are, therefore, committed to evangelism, healing, deliverance, discipleship and training. The particular scriptures on which our mission is founded are Isaiah 61:1–7; Matthew 28:18–20; Luke 9:1–2; 9:11; Ephesians 4:12; 2 Timothy 2:2.

Our Basis of Faith
God is a Trinity. God the Father loves all people. God the Son, Jesus Christ, is Saviour and Healer, Lord and King. God the Holy Spirit indwells Christians and imparts the dynamic power by which they are enabled to continue Christ's ministry. The Bible is the divinely inspired authority in matters of faith, doctrine and conduct, and is the basis for teaching.

For details about the current worldwide activities of Ellel Ministries International please go to: www.ellel.org
Ellel Ministries International
Ellel Grange
Ellel
Lancaster, LA2 0HN
United Kingdom
Tel (+44) (0)1524 751 651

Other books in this series

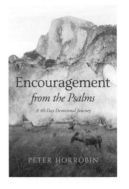

Encouragement from the Psalms
There are times in all our lives when we need encouragement. Encouragement enables us to look up instead of down and gives us the determination to keep going whatever our circumstances. God is a great encourager, as David discovered throughout his years of seeking to walk in God's ways. These devotionals, which are built around key verses in the Psalms, reflect on how God encouraged David and provide daily encouragement for Christian believers today.
144 pages, RRP £9.99
ISBN 978-1-85240-801-5
Available Autumn 2018

Comfort from God's Heart
Paul referred to God as *'the God of ALL comfort'*. Meaning that whatever our situation or circumstances God wants to be our ultimate source of comfort. And Jesus also said, *"Blessed are those that mourn, for they shall be comforted"*. But it's not just at times of mourning that we need comfort. Life can deliver some hard blows and unless we learn to turn

to God for the comfort we need, we may be tempted to find our comfort in all the wrong places. This devotional volume draws on many different parts of the Bible to deliver a message of comfort from the heart of God.

144 pages,
ISBN 978-1-85240-816-9
Available Spring 2019

Wisdom from the Proverbs

Where do we go for help, when we need God's wisdom? Our primary source of wisdom must be the Word of God. And within the Bible, the book which encapsulates a wealth of pithy wisdom is the book of Proverbs. Spurgeon referred to the Proverbs as a salt-cellar, from which the Holy Spirit sprinkles the wisdom of God on the life of believers. This devotional volume provides a rich source of wisdom to feed the soul and encourage the spirit.

144 pages,
ISBN 978-1-85240-831-2

Would You Join With Us To Bless the Nations?

At the Sovereign World Trust, our mandate and passion is to send books, like the one you've just read, to *faithful leaders who can equip others* (2 Tim 2:2).

The 'Good News' is that in all of the poorest nations we reach, the Kingdom of God is growing in an accelerated way but, to further this Great Commission work, the Pastors and Leaders in these countries need good teaching resources in order to provide sound Biblical doctrine to their flock, their future generations and especially new converts.

If you could donate a copy of this or other titles from Sovereign World Ltd, you will be helping to supply much-needed resources to Pastors and Leaders in many countries.

Contact us for more information on (+44)(0)1732 851150 or visit our website www.sovereignworldtrust.org.uk

> *"I have all it takes to further my studies. Sovereign is making it all possible for me"*
>
> **Rev. Akfred Keyas – Kenya**

> *"My ministry is rising up gradually since I have been teaching people from these books"*
>
> **Pastor John Obaseki – Nigeria**